NATIONAL ACADEMIES Sciences Engineering Medicine

I0794841

NATIONAL ACADEMIES PRESS
Washington, DC

Foundations of Data Science for Students in Grades K–12

Erin Hammers Forstag, *Rapporteur*

Board on Science Education

Division of Behavioral and Social Sciences and Education

Proceedings of a Workshop

NATIONAL ACADEMIES PRESS 500 Fifth Street, NW, Washington, DC 20001

This activity was supported by contracts between the National Academy of Sciences and the Valhalla Foundation (unnumbered) and the President's Committee Funds. Any opinions, findings, conclusions, or recommendations expressed in this publication do not necessarily reflect the views of any organization or agency that provided support for the project.

International Standard Book Number-13: 978-0-309-69815-3
International Standard Book Number-10: 0-309-69815-4
Digital Object Identifier: https://doi.org/10.17226/26852

This publication is available from the National Academies Press, 500 Fifth Street, NW, Keck 360, Washington, DC 20001; (800) 624-6242 or (202) 334-3313; http://www.nap.edu.

Printed in the United States of America.

Suggested citation: National Academies of Sciences, Engineering, and Medicine. 2023. *Foundations of Data Science for Students in Grades K–12: Proceedings of a Workshop*. Washington, DC: The National Academies Press. https://doi.org/10.17226/26852.

The **National Academy of Sciences** was established in 1863 by an Act of Congress, signed by President Lincoln, as a private, nongovernmental institution to advise the nation on issues related to science and technology. Members are elected by their peers for outstanding contributions to research. Dr. Marcia McNutt is president.

The **National Academy of Engineering** was established in 1964 under the charter of the National Academy of Sciences to bring the practices of engineering to advising the nation. Members are elected by their peers for extraordinary contributions to engineering. Dr. John L. Anderson is president.

The **National Academy of Medicine** (formerly the Institute of Medicine) was established in 1970 under the charter of the National Academy of Sciences to advise the nation on medical and health issues. Members are elected by their peers for distinguished contributions to medicine and health. Dr. Victor J. Dzau is president.

The three Academies work together as the **National Academies of Sciences, Engineering, and Medicine** to provide independent, objective analysis and advice to the nation and conduct other activities to solve complex problems and inform public policy decisions. The National Academies also encourage education and research, recognize outstanding contributions to knowledge, and increase public understanding in matters of science, engineering, and medicine.

Learn more about the National Academies of Sciences, Engineering, and Medicine at **www.nationalacademies.org**.

Consensus Study Reports published by the National Academies of Sciences, Engineering, and Medicine document the evidence-based consensus on the study's statement of task by an authoring committee of experts. Reports typically include findings, conclusions, and recommendations based on information gathered by the committee and the committee's deliberations. Each report has been subjected to a rigorous and independent peer-review process and it represents the position of the National Academies on the statement of task.

Proceedings published by the National Academies of Sciences, Engineering, and Medicine chronicle the presentations and discussions at a workshop, symposium, or other event convened by the National Academies. The statements and opinions contained in proceedings are those of the participants and are not endorsed by other participants, the planning committee, or the National Academies.

Rapid Expert Consultations published by the National Academies of Sciences, Engineering, and Medicine are authored by subject-matter experts on narrowly focused topics that can be supported by a body of evidence. The discussions contained in rapid expert consultations are considered those of the authors and do not contain policy recommendations. Rapid expert consultations are reviewed by the institution before release.

For information about other products and activities of the National Academies, please visit www.nationalacademies.org/about/whatwedo.

PLANNING COMMITTEE FOR FOUNDATIONS OF DATA SCIENCE FOR STUDENTS IN GRADES K–12: A WORKSHOP

NICHOLAS J. HORTON (*Co-Chair*), Amherst College
MICHELLE H. WILKERSON (*Co-Chair*), University of California, Berkeley
TAMARA L. CLEGG, University of Maryland
ZAREK D. DROZDA, Data Science 4 Everyone
TIMOTHY E. ERICKSON, Epistemological Engineering
HOLLYLYNNE STOHL LEE, North Carolina State University
CAMILLIA MATUK, New York University
LEIGH F. PEAKE, Gulf of Maine Research Institute

Staff

AMY STEPHENS, *Study Director,* Board on Science Education
JANET GAO, *Program Officer,* Board on Science Education
LAUREN RYAN, *Senior Program Assistant,* Board on Science Education
HEIDI SCHWEINGRUBER, *Director,* Board on Science Education

Acknowledgments

This Proceedings of a Workshop was reviewed in draft form by individuals chosen for their diverse perspectives and technical expertise. The purpose of this independent review is to provide candid and critical comments that will assist the National Academies of Sciences, Engineering, and Medicine in making each published proceedings as sound as possible and to ensure that it meets the institutional standards for quality, objectivity, evidence, and responsiveness to the charge. The review comments and draft manuscript remain confidential to protect the integrity of the process.

We thank the following individuals for their review of this proceedings: Andres Henriquez, Education Development Center, Inc.; Rachel Levy, North Carolina State University; and Andee Rubin, TERC.

Although the reviewers listed above provided many constructive comments and suggestions, they were not asked to endorse the content of the proceedings nor did they see the final draft before its release. The review of this proceedings was overseen by Marcia C. Linn, University of California, Berkeley. She was responsible for making certain that an independent examination of this proceedings was carried out in accordance with standards of the National Academies and that all review comments were carefully considered. Responsibility for the final content rests entirely with the rapporteur and the National Academies.

Contents

Boxes, Figures, and Table

BOXES

FIGURES

TABLE

1

Introduction

On September 13 and 14, 2022, the Board on Science Education at the National Academies of Sciences, Engineering, and Medicine held a workshop entitled "Foundations of Data Science for Students in Grades K–12." Speakers and participants joined the workshop both in-person in Washington, D.C., and virtually via Zoom. Heidi Schweingruber, director of the Board on Science Education, welcomed participants to the workshop and gave a brief overview of previous work conducted by the National Academies related to the topic. Over a decade ago, she said, *A Framework for K–12 Science Education* (National Research Council, 2012) was published; this report called out the importance of mathematics and data analysis. A National Academies of Sciences, Engineering, and Medicine 2018 report, *Data Science for Undergraduates*, catalyzed conversations around data science education in K–12. If data science is important in undergraduate school, "why aren't we attending to what we're doing in K–12?" asked Schweingruber. Other activities and reports that led to this workshop include *STEM Integration in K–12 Education* (2014), *Cultivating Interest and Competencies in Computing* (2021), and the Roundtable on Data Science Postsecondary Education.[1] Work around data science has been accelerating quickly, she said, and this workshop presents an opportunity for stakeholders to discuss different ideas in a collaborative way.

Co-chair Michelle Wilkerson (University of California, Berkeley) highlighted that the workshop was designed to draw attention to the rapidly

[1]https://www.nationalacademies.org/our-work/roundtable-on-data-science-postsecondary-education#:~:text=The%20Roundtable%20on%20Data%20Science,and%20ways%20to%20move%20forward

growing field of K–12 data science education by surveying the current landscape; surfacing what is known; and identifying what is needed to support student learning, develop curriculum and tools, and prepare educators (see Box 1-1). Speakers and participants at the workshop included researchers and practitioners engaged in K–12 data science education from a variety of contexts, including formal and informal; designed and emergent; elementary and secondary; and whose efforts include standalone curricula as well as activities integrated within other content areas (e.g., science, technology, engineering, and mathematics [STEM] disciplines and the humanities). Wilkerson noted that the emphasis of the first day would be on visioning and outcomes whereas the discussions the second day would dig in more concretely to what K–12 data science education looks like in practice. To support these conversations, said Wilkerson, four papers were commissioned and discussed during the workshop:

1. A Secret Agent: K–12 Data Science Learning Through the Lens of Agency[2]
2. Critical Data Literacy: Creating a More Just World Through Data[3]
3. Previewing the National Landscape of K–12 Data Science Implementation[4]
4. Tools to Support Data Analysis and Data Science in K–12 Education[5]

This workshop is a "rare and exciting opportunity," said co-chair Nicholas Horton (Amherst College). Data science in K–12 education is in its infancy, and participants at the workshop have the opportunity to think creatively about how it can best serve students and future citizens. Horton shared four opportunities and challenges that lie ahead for K–12 data science:

1. It is critical that stakeholders act now to ensure that the disparities seen in STEM are not replicated in data science. All students, said Horton, need access to high-quality programs in order to explore and make sense of the data around them.

---

[2]https://www.nationalacademies.org/event/09-13-2022/docs/DD667E469D0EC5DD91A7D85BC839A9852491A3CF9F15

[3]https://www.nationalacademies.org/event/09-13-2022/docs/D16254F310D01BBDA873920E4EFB8151F2D8334181AA

[4]https://www.nationalacademies.org/event/09-13-2022/docs/D688ED916E82498DA0E2171A109936D679FD5DE26556

[5]https://www.nationalacademies.org/documents/embed/link/LF2255DA3DD1C41C0A42D3BEF0989ACAECE3053A6A9B/file/DB48F8A34F71C395C3071BABFFD42AFFF06478824419

BOX 1-1
Statement of Task

The National Academies of Sciences, Engineering, and Medicine will convene a public workshop of the *Foundations of Data Science for Students in Grades K–12*. The workshop will explore questions, such as the following:

Goals and outcomes

- What outcomes matter most for learners?
- What competencies make up data fluency?
- How can these data fluency competencies be measured?

Tools and instruction

- What kinds of learning experiences might help bring about these data fluency competencies?
- What tools and data sets are needed to support young learners in acquiring data understanding and skills?
- How can K–12 data science education be designed to specifically reach students who have been traditionally marginalized and/or underrepresented in STEM?

Integrating data science into the K–12 system

- How can data science be meaningfully integrated with K–12 education, in both STEM and non-STEM classes?
- How well prepared is the current teacher workforce for teaching data science-related content in K–12 settings? What strategies could be used to enhance teachers' expertise related to data science?

The evidence base and future directions

- What bodies of research can be leveraged to gain insight on the development of data fluency and how best to support students?
- What are the critical gaps in the current knowledge base?
- What are the highest priority next steps for research and practice?

2. There are a plethora of powerful tools and technologies available; however, it is an open question what role these should play in teaching, learning, and lessening disparities. For example, he said, cloud computing and open-source tools have the potential to improve access and lessen disparities, but this will only happen if the technologies are deployed appropriately.
3. There is a need to think about which educational pathways are most promising, and how general knowledge of student learning and development can inform practice in this area.

4. The implementation of effective K–12 data science education will require confident, prepared teachers who have a foundation in data acumen.[6] The COVID-19 pandemic exacerbated challenges in teacher recruitment, training, and retention, and it is critical that these challenges be addressed.

Horton then offered a list of guiding questions for workshop participants to keep in mind during the workshop presentations and discussions (see Box 1-2).

Horton noted that although these questions were not likely to be answered in full over the two days, he hoped that the workshop would shed light on possible answers, spur fruitful discussions, and connect stakeholders and different communities.

REPORT ORGANIZATION

This proceedings summarizes the presentations and discussions highlighted during the workshop. Proceedings may not contain any consensus analysis or views of the committee on the underlying subject matter of the workshop. This proceedings may contain particular viewpoints attributed to individual participants or groups of participants in the workshop, if

BOX 1-2
Workshop Guiding Questions

- What does data science education look like? Where is it happening, both in and out of school?
- How can data science education be designed so that it:
  - Prepares all students to access, learn, and practice data science;
  - Invites and supports diversity in who participates in data science, including along the dimensions of race/ethnicity, gender, and disability status; and
  - Encourages more just and ethical approaches to data science as a field?
- Where should data science education be located?
- What is special about data science?
- What is special about doing data science in K–12?
- How can the somewhat siloed communities involved in this space come together to collaborate, learn, and share findings?

[6] "Data acumen" is a phrase used to describe some of the specific skills needed for data science. There are a few different meanings associated with this term but no agreed upon working definition in K–12.

these attributions can be adequately documented and if the viewpoints are reasonable statements for inclusion in a National Academies proceedings. Chapter 2 explores the vision for data science education in K–12: What is it that we want students to be able to do with data, and how can we assess and measure the intended outcomes? Chapter 3 looks at the current landscape of data science education, and features speakers working on the ground and in the classroom. Chapter 4 discusses the tools, resources, and teacher preparation that are needed to implement the vision of data science education, and Chapter 5 looks toward the future by identifying priorities for research and funding.

2

Vision for K–12 Data Science Education and Outcomes

Data science is in its infancy, and there is an opportunity to shape it in a way that will best serve students and future citizens. Given this early stage, there is a need to think deeply and creatively about how data science looks within K–12 and how it might develop in ways that do not replicate the disparities observed in other fields and disciplines. Moreover, to ensure that all students have access to high-quality programs and are able to make sense of the data around them, sessions were designed around the following questions: Why are we interested in data science at the K–12 level? What outcomes do we want for students, for the practice of data science education, etc.?

CREATING A VISION OF "HIGH-QUALITY" K–12 DATA SCIENCE EDUCATION

In this session of the workshop, speakers and participants explored what defines a valuable learning experience for students, what research has revealed about successful and unsuccessful curricular interventions, and how these learnings can be articulated into policy and practice. M. Wilkerson moderated the session by posing a series of questions to the panelists. A Q&A session with workshop participants followed the moderated session.

Importance of Data Science Education

Why do we think data science education is important? Why are we all here today?

The level of data knowledge that is now required is "historically high," said Rob Gould (University of California, Los Angeles). For example, the *p* value crisis in the statistics world[1] demonstrates the need to adequately prepare students and practitioners to understand and use the fundamental tools of data analysis. Undergraduate students are coming into college with no foundation to build on, he said, which makes teaching introductory statistics challenging. At the same time, we live in a world where nearly every interaction—both personal and professional—is mediated through data. This situation presents both "perils and promises," said Gould. The peril is that ignorance of data is harmful to individuals and society. The promise is that even a small amount of knowledge about how to make sense of data and how to communicate about them can be "tremendously empowering." It is critical to begin to develop data acumen at the youngest ages and to include all students in these efforts. At this point, he said, "we are a long way from building [data knowledge] successfully and at the level that we require."

Josh Recio (Dana Center) agreed and added that the way math education has been conducted has historically excluded and harmed some students, specifically Black, Latino, and lower-income students. The one-size-fits-all approach to math education has sent a message to these students that they do not belong and that they cannot be a "math person." To address this issue and to reach all students with data literacy efforts, he said, it is essential that math education be presented in a relevant and useful way. For example, if students can see explicit links between math education and the world around them, they may be encouraged to see themselves as "math people" and pursue further education in the area. Recio said that data science presents an opportunity to make these types of linkages for students, and that using data science to make math more relevant makes it possible to change the message about "who belongs in math courses and who can be successful."

There are three overwhelmingly important reasons to address data science in K–12 education, said Alfred Spector (Massachusetts Institute of Technology). First, our ability to sense, process, and promulgate data has changed the world, and this trend will continue to accelerate and have an enormous impact. With this as the backdrop, said Spector, data science is a critical part of K–12 education. Second, data science is informed and used by a wide variety of disciplines; incorporating data science into education provides an opportunity to challenge students and

---

[1]For more information, see Amrhein and colleagues (2019).

enrich disciplinary education. Third, data science—including the use of computational models—is becoming ever more dominant. Whether students eventually go into computer science, STEM, health, public policy, economics, or other fields, Spector concluded, there is a need for everyone to be able to understand and critically think about the use of data and the conclusions drawn from these data.

The Next Generation Science Standards (NGSS),[2] said Tricia Shelton (National Science Teaching Association), do not address data science specifically. However, they emphasize that students are expected to explain their world, to develop scientific explanations, and to design solutions to problems. As other speakers have noted, the problems and phenomena of our world are now complex and often involve large amounts of data. Empowering children to make sense of the rapidly changing and complex world can give them agency and an ability to be critical consumers and critical decision makers. By integrating data science into all disciplines—not just science—students will be prepared to have an impact in whatever they choose to do. Today's K–12 students are the future leaders of our world, added Trena Wilkerson (Baylor University; National Council of Teachers of Mathematics). Helping students to understand and be able to use and critique data science is critical for giving them a voice and preparing them to lead.

Identifying "Success" for K–12 Data Science Education

Given these reasons for why data science education is important, how can we be sure we are doing it well? What does it mean to be successfully educating students in terms of what they learn? Who ends up participating in data science, and what will data science look like in the future?

Spector noted the "dual nature" of data science education. One side is the mathematical, computational aspect of data science; the other is understanding the role of data and how to think critically about data. The second aspect is extremely important for all students and can be infused across all disciplines. Data are widely available, but unfortunately, he said, there is "very little understanding and care" about the proper use of data, (e.g., the difference between correlation and causation). Spector mused that improper use of data to "make a point" is one of the reasons for the divisiveness in society today. There are ample opportunities throughout the K–12 curriculum to draw attention to this issue and to teach students about data. Whether students are preparing to enter STEM fields, pursuing other educational degrees, or entering the workforce after high school, data science education is critical to provide them with fundamental tools.

---

[2]For more information, see https://www.nextgenscience.org/

One of the driving motivations for teaching data science in K–12 is the need for a data-literate workforce, said Recio. Ten or 15 years in the future, he said, we will be able to assess these efforts by looking at whether employees and students in higher education are coming in with the preparation and knowledge they need to succeed. However, he said, it will also be clear that efforts in this area have failed if there are clear lines between students who benefited and students who were harmed, in particular if there are lines between racial/ethnic groups or between income groups. It is important, said Recio, to carefully consider what is defined as "success" and for whom. T. Wilkerson added that one way to monitor whether data science education efforts are successful is to look at the pathways that are developed. She explained that pathways that carry students from pre-K through higher education could be inclusive and ensure that all students have opportunities or could create further barriers and reify structural issues. There is a need to continually assess the pathways for data science education to find what is working and what is not working; this assessment is particularly important because data science cuts across all disciplines.

Opportunities for Data Science in K–12 Education

Where does data science fit in K–12? Does it fit in STEM or other courses, or how should it be integrated?

"Data science should be integrated everywhere," said Shelton. Two of the key elements in science education are relevance and authenticity, she said; studying complex and relevant phenomena helps to keep students engaged and interested. When considering data science education, the approach should be the same. When data science is integrated with other disciplines, and the questions about data are interesting and relevant to students, "magic in a classroom" can happen. One way to accomplish this, said Shelton, is to partner with those who have expertise in data science to develop instructional materials and approaches for integrating data science in the classroom.

Gould noted that although data science can be integrated across disciplines, it is also critical to focus on the "fundamental core" of data science. Looking at data science can be like looking at an elephant, he said; people from different disciplines and industries may all see a different part of the elephant. When implementing data science education into K–12, there is a need to focus on the essential ideas and approaches that apply to all disciplines. Gould argued that data science needs to be presented as a "subject worthy of itself" as well as explored in the context of other subjects.

Implications for Policy and Action

What recommendations do you have for this workshop? What should be done?

One critical step, said Gould, is to build bridges to the university level. If a high school student takes a statistics course, how does this course fit in with future studies in college? Are there opportunities for students to build on their learning and integrate it into coursework in computer programming, the use of algorithms, and problem solving? Gould said there is a need to build a curricular bridge between K–12 and higher education, and to develop clear and explicit pathways for learning. There is also a need to build a bridge across the K–12 grade levels; although there are courses, he said, we need a coherent scaffold.

The interdisciplinary nature of data science, said Recio, demands "a collective movement." Stakeholders across multiple disciplines and from the education community, the workforce, and practitioners need to work together to organize and communicate about how to move data science education forward. Further, these stakeholders need to bring what they've learned back to their own institutions and push for change. T. Wilkerson challenged workshop participants to consider two areas in which progress needs to be made. First, which of the stakeholders and collaborators need to be brought into conversations? How could bringing in the voices of community members, families, students, and others help move data science forward? Second, said T. Wilkerson, it is critical to examine policies and practices that are inhibiting these efforts, and to identify ways to eliminate or mitigate them. For example, K–12 educators are unlikely to have the time necessary to sit down and collaborate and develop data science curriculum; mitigating this challenge may require providing teachers with more time or engaging more stakeholders in the process. Shelton added that professional learning will be a critical part of implementing data science education in K–12; research has found that many science teachers are hesitant and uncomfortable with the topic. Partnerships between science educators and those with expertise in data science can also be essential in supporting educators in moving data science forward, she said. In those partnerships, everyone is both "learner" and "contributor," bringing both the science expertise as well as learning more about data science and vice versa.

In considering how to move data science forward, Spector encouraged workshop participants to use a "divide and conquer" method. Focusing on making progress on specific smaller goals may be easier than trying to solve every problem simultaneously, he said. For example, there are a large number of teachers who are untrained, educational districts have different requirements, and parents and communities have their own views and priorities for education; solving these issues simultaneously would be "quite hard." One area in which there is tremendous opportunity, said Spector, is in using computational technologies to make education immersive, adaptive, and "actually fun." Although technology cannot solve every curricular issue, there is an opportunity to infuse data, analysis, programming, and statistics into the curriculum to improve efficiency and learning.

Audience Q&A

How are we defining "data science"? How does it relate to data literacy? Is data science its own emerging discipline or a set of tools that lives across multiple disciplines?

There is a false dichotomy between teaching data literacy and data science, said Gould. Before teaching data science—and specific tools such as machine learning—students need a foundational understanding in data literacy. Teaching the skills before the understanding, he said, is "putting the cart before the horse." Gould noted that he prefers the term "data acumen" rather than "data literacy." Spector added that while data science has become its own discipline, it is built upon multiple other disciplines. Although it is important to teach a holistic and unified view of data science, it is also critical to provide opportunities for students to gain an in-depth understanding of the underlying disciplines (e.g., statistics, computation).

Given the siloed nature of courses in middle and high school, how do we ensure that data science occurs across all disciplines in parallel with learning the basics of statistics and data analysis? How can all teachers participate in adding elements of data science into their teaching?

T. Wilkerson responded that data science is a "perfect venue" for collaboration across disciplines. Although this type of collaboration is unfortunately not common, it is essential in this area to show students the transdisciplinary nature and importance of data science. To facilitate collaboration, time and opportunities for collaboration need to be provided to teachers throughout their training and careers. Recio added that moving data science forward will require investing in teachers; teachers need training and time to learn how to teach data science and to understand the ultimate goal for students. "If we don't make that investment" in preservice and in-service training, said Recio, we will struggle to implement data science in K–12 education.

How do we address the tension between the rapidly changing world of data and technology, and the slow-to-change world of education?

Although technology itself changes quickly, said Gould, the fundamentals do not. Recio agreed and said that he is often asked which programming language teachers should use in the classroom and his answer is that it doesn't matter. Technologies are constantly changing but exposing students to any technology will help them moving forward. He added, however, that it is important to prepare teachers to be able to confidently work with available technologies and tools, and that they need continuous learning and support in this area. Gould said that the "elephant in the room" is the cost of technologies; obtaining and updating technology for the classroom is "extraordinarily expensive."

A VISION FOR K–12 DATA SCIENCE LEARNING AND OUTCOMES

This session of the workshop was designed to explore evidence on learning and critical data literacy to consider what students should be able to do with data and how outcomes should be measured. Before the start of the session, participants were broken up into small groups to discuss outcomes for data science education. Discussions centered on both student-level outcomes (e.g., developing specific skills and proficiencies, developing interest or disciplinary identity) and outcomes related to policy and practice (e.g., access to opportunities, funding). The session, moderated by Horton, included two invited speakers and commentary by an invited panelist, followed by discussion with workshop participants including a summary of the small group conversations.

K–12 Data Science Learning Through the Lens of Agency[3]

"What do we know about data science learning?" asked Ryan "Seth" Jones, Middle Tennessee State University. This is a difficult question to answer for two reasons. First, data science is an emergent and diverse field. Many different communities are generating and revising knowledge using data science ideas and practices, and technologies and methods change quickly. Second, research on data science learning is happening in diverse contexts, including K–12 classrooms and undergraduate classrooms, and across diverse theoretical traditions. For these reasons, Jones said, it may be difficult to synthesize the research on student learning.

Jones told workshop participants about what he and his colleague found when examining the body of research on student learning. Through the landscape review, of the papers identified, it was found that researchers in this area privilege different types of agency within data science learning: material agency, personal agency, and disciplinary agency. Material agency,

[3]For more information about the methods and resources described throughout the presentation, see https://www.nationalacademies.org/event/09-13-2022/docs/DD667E469D0EC5DD91A7D85BC839A9852491A3CF9F15

Jones explained, reflects the idea that the world does things and is "hard to wrangle." He noted that this includes worlds that emerge from computing tools. Personal agency describes the way that individual people respond to the world, whereas disciplinary agency occurs when communities create a new form of collective agency that constrains the choices of individuals. Jones clarified that these are not mutually exclusive categories, but that in general, most studies highlight one type of agency over the others.

Studies that highlight material agency, said Jones, place emphasis on the role of data science in giving students the opportunity to learn fundamental ideas about variability, measurement, sampling, etc. Material agency supports learners to understand the context through which data came to be, and it can be productive for students to describe sources of variability, including variability due to measurement, the phenomenon under investigation, and random noise. Studies that focus on the role of personal agency, in contrast, highlight different aspects of learning. First, they recognize that learners possess epistemic (knowledge-related) assets and that it is important to recognize these assets. Second, these studies focus on the ways in which students can be positioned to see data as personally meaningful, can construct coherent data stories, and can develop data science approaches that resemble disciplinary approaches in meaningful ways. Jones noted that personal agency is not a "magic bullet." It takes a lot of work to design environments and to scaffold and sequence learning so that learners can exert personal agency and also make progress toward generating answers to the questions on which they are working. Finally, said Jones, research that prioritizes disciplinary agency emphasizes the roles of computing and highly valued disciplinary procedures and tools. For example, many studies examine specific programming languages that are valued in the discipline (e.g., R and Python). These studies find that students can learn to use particular tools valued in a discipline when supported through careful instructional design.

Examining these different types of agency, said Jones, led to several questions and considerations about how to move forward with the work of K–12 data science education:

- Should different forms of agency be prioritized depending on where the work is oriented?
- What is the role of systems-level organizations and support to synthesize the work?
- What new communities and voices are needed?
- How much weight should be given to the different dimensions of data science learning?
- Whose voice is highlighted in research on data science learning?

Critical Data Literacy: Creating a More Just World with Data[4]

People have long called for stronger data literacy in the general population, said Josephine Louie (Education Development Center, Inc. [EDC]). Large-scale surveys of business managers and the public have found that up to 80 percent of people have little confidence in their abilities to make sense of data. We now live in a world of "big data," she said, which presents new questions about privacy and power. Powerful actors are collecting massive amounts of data from the public constantly, with or without consent, and these data are used to predict and modify behavior. Many writers have described the harms that arise when our data are used to decide "who we are, what we will buy, where we will go, what we will do, what messages we will gravitate toward, and what we will believe." Within this context, said Louie, there are growing calls for critical data literacy.

General data literacy is anchored in statistical literacy and requires an understanding of and fluency with the data investigation process (Figure 2-1). This process involves formulating questions that can be answered with data, assembling data to address these questions, using statistical and other tools to analyze the data, drawing inferences, summarizing conclusions, and communicating findings to various audiences. Data literacy also involves familiarity with multivariable data and reasoning, said Louie, because large-scale data and social and natural phenomena are multivariable. In addition, the process involves constant questioning throughout all stages about the "who, what, when, where, and why" surrounding the data. Notions of internal and external validity of any claims based on data depend on answers to all of these questions, she said.

In the world of big data, there is a need to expand beyond these statistical foundations. Critical data literacy expands on data literacy to include an understanding of when and how data are collected from us, an understanding of algorithms and what they do, and a consideration of the ethical impacts of data collection and data-based decisions. Further, critical data literacy requires awareness of unequal power structures in society and how data can be used to perpetuate or worsen social inequality.[5] Louie said that "there is a tradition in educational research and practice that looks critically at unjust structures in society and the role that education and data may play in questioning and countering these structures to create a more just world." Applying these ideas, said Louie, critical data literacy can be seen as "learning to read and write the world with data." Reading the world

---

[4]For more information about the methods and resources described throughout the presentation, see https://www.nationalacademies.org/event/09-13-2022/docs/D16254F310D01BBDA873920E4EFB8151F2D83341 81AA

[5]Books such as *Data Feminism*, *Weapons of Math Destruction*, and *Algorithms of Oppression* make these arguments.

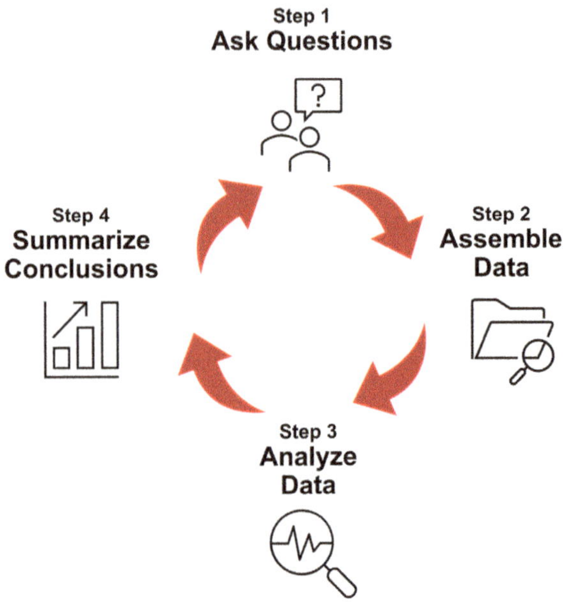

FIGURE 2-1 A simple representation of the data investigation process.
SOURCE: Presentation by Jo Louie, September 13, 2022.

with data, explained Louie, could mean using data to raise students' critical consciousness of social and political inequalities in the world. Writing the world with data could mean helping students to build social agency to take action, both individually and collectively, against unjust social arrangements. Part of this work, said Louie, is using data to help non-dominant groups build pride in their own cultural and social identities.

Louie described some takeaways from a commissioned paper she wrote for the workshop.[6] In the paper, she highlighted eight examples of interventions aimed at promoting critical data literacy in K–12 education. Four of the studies, she said, could be seen as helping students to read the world with data. Several of these studies took place in middle and high school mathematics classes, where students examined large-scale social and economic datasets to uncover persistent and large-scale patterns of inequality in housing, income, and the local lottery. Another study took place in a high school summer technology program; students were able to read the social media posts and private information of everyone within a

[6]https://www.nationalacademies.org/event/09-13-2022/docs/D16254F310D01BBDA87 3920E4EFB8151F2D8334181AA

specific geographic location, allowing them to see how technologies can violate people's privacy. The other four studies, said Louie, could be seen as helping students write the world with data. These studies took place in science classes, social studies classes, media art classes, and a public library. Students used data to envision and propose how to improve local public spaces, to craft and relay stories about their own family histories, and to share an aspect of their own personal lives expressed artistically through the design of t-shirts. Outcomes reported by these studies included more critical perspectives of society and awareness of different forms of social and economic inequality, greater agency in authoring with data, and greater feelings of power to shape and control what data are shared or hidden.

These studies also reported that there were challenges involved in promoting critical data literacy, said Louie. For example, critical sociopolitical views may not arise naturally or easily, due to student resistance and persistence of existing views. In addition, discussing social and political inequality can be difficult, with the potential for invoking feelings of disempowerment and negative stereotypes of non-dominant groups. These discussions can be particularly harmful to students when teachers are not trained in how to conduct them well, she said.

In conclusion, Louie said that learning to read and write the world with data may be a helpful framework for promoting critical data literacy because reading and writing with text are already fundamental and familiar goals in K–12 education. The examples that Louie provided suggest promise in using data to build awareness of unequal social structures and build agency in authoring one's own stories and social visions. However, questions and considerations remain. First, most studies did not report a strong focus on quantitative reasoning. If critical data literacy can be separated from quantitative reasoning, she said, we need to consider how it differs from critical information literacy or critical media literacy. If these competencies cannot be separated, there is a need for a framework that builds both competencies in a coordinated manner. Second, Louie said that promoting critical data literacy is an interdisciplinary effort, and there is a need for spaces and support for educators to work across disciplines. Third, most of the examples that Louie found were with small groups of students. If critical data literacy is important, there is a need to find ways to scale up interventions and tools to assess progress. Finally, said Louie, there is a need to determine whether and how interventions designed for certain groups will need to be adapted for other groups. For example, she said, there may be resistance among White students or parents when data are used to critique existing power structures.

Panelist Reflection: K–12 Data Science Learning and Assessment

Following the presentations by Jones and Louie, Jo Boaler (Stanford University) offered her reflections on the topics discussed and how they related to the issue of assessment. Boaler concurred that the presentations covered topics that are essential aspects of data science. A framework of agency highlights the importance of students asking questions, building models, interpreting data, and communicating, whereas critical data literacy focuses on students' ability to understand and shape their world using data. When considering how to assess the effectiveness of data science education, said Boaler, it is important to capture these competencies and practices rather than simply assessing content knowledge. For example, she said, it is fairly simple to evaluate a student's knowledge of statistics, programming, or multivariate reasoning. However, concepts like agency and critical data literacy are "the essence of data science" and if assessments do not capture these practices, she said, they will misrepresent data science and threaten the achievement of equitable outcomes.

Assessments that focus on capturing practices rather than merely content knowledge are critical to equity, said Boaler. For example, a large part of the variance in SAT math scores is predicted by race, once achievement is factored out. In contrast, the Smarter Balanced[7] assessment for mathematics (which permits the use of a calculator) captures the ability to reason and use mathematical practices. When this assessment is used instead of the SAT, it results in a more socioeconomically and racially diverse group of students going forward. These assessments "really matter," she said. For assessments to capture the "essence" of data science and to prioritize equitable outcomes, assessments must capture practices and competencies such as agency and critical literacy rather than merely evaluating content knowledge, said Boaler.

Participant Report Out and Q&A with Panelists

Following the reflections from Boaler, a subset of workshop participants discussed their conversations, asked questions of the panelists (Jones, Louie, and Boaler), and reflected on emerging themes. To set the stage for discussion, workshop participants contributed their answers to the question: "What are some desired outcomes for K–12 data science education?" A word cloud was made with their answers (Figure 2-2).

Zarek Drozda (Data Science 4 Everyone, University of Chicago) began by summarizing themes that emerged from his group's discussion. First, he said, several group members emphasized the importance of explicating

[7]https://smarterbalanced.org/

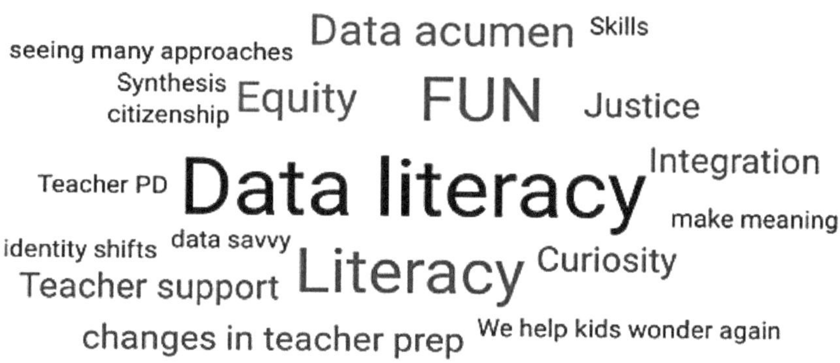

FIGURE 2-2 Word cloud of workshop participant answers for the desired outcomes for K–12 data science education.
SOURCE: Generated at workshop, September 13, 2022.

the motivations for teaching data science so that they can be critiqued and adapted over time. Second, multiple individuals stated that data science is essential not only for students entering tech careers but for all students to be educated and productive members of society. Students need to be able to understand how and when data are collected, how to analyze and critique data visualizations, and how to use data to make decisions and shape their world. M. Wilkerson shared two insights from her group. First, individuals discussed the importance of developing assessments that capture a broad range of student outcomes. Second, there was discussion about how to ensure that interested students are prepared to pursue data science at the college level, while not prematurely cutting off other students from pursuing this path. One idea that was floated, said M. Wilkerson, was developing summer bridge programs at universities to ensure preparedness. Horton commented that this idea points to the need for collaboration and coordination of data science curricula across multiple levels of education.

Relationship to Other Education Movements

A virtual workshop participant commented that if you look at computer science standards, the end goal is often working with real-world data; she asked whether this goal is consistent with the goals of the data science education movement. Horton said that whereas some aspects of computational thinking are different from aspects of data science, there is a "lot of overlap" and the ideas are often mutually reinforcing. Drozda added that there are opportunities for collaboration between computer science and data science; for example, a computer science educator can serve as a resource for other teachers to help with programming. Creating more explicit spaces for collaboration between educators working in related fields will be critical for moving data science forward, he said. Jones agreed and said that other fields, like science and mathematics, often have specific practices or ideas for developing competencies in students, and that data science education could lean on these experiences.

Louie said that her journey in data science has always been based in real-world data. For her, data was a way for her to understand her identity and how she fits into the world. One of Louie's projects involves bringing the U.S. Census, particularly American Community Survey data, into math and social studies classes in order for students to ask questions and engage with the data. Louie said that the students in these classes—many of whom are immigrants and/or from non-dominant communities—welcomed the opportunity to learn about issues such as income inequality and immigration. Many said it was the best class they'd ever taken, said Louie, because the data are being used to answer questions and delve into topics they care about.

Indigenous Data

Eileen Manchester (Library of Congress) shared some information and resources about Indigenous data sovereignty. She said that this topic is critical for those working in data science education and encouraged workshop participants to read works by scholars including Stephanie Russo Carroll, Desi Rodriguez Lonebear, Lynn Lavalley, Eve Tuck, and Linda Tuhiwai Smith. These works, she explained, explore the issue of Indigenous and tribal groups having control over the data that are collected about them and retaining governance over such data.

Relationship to Citizen Science

The ideas explored in this workshop, said Allissa Dillman (Biodata Sage), echo the concept of "citizen science." Citizen science projects, she explained, involve students going into their communities, collecting data, interpreting the results, and potentially advocating for changes. For example, a group of middle school students in Maine tested arsenic levels in their community water and testified in the state senate in favor of action. Louie commented that the idea of citizen science is related to the discussions around agency. In a citizen science project, there are multiple opportunities for students to have agency over asking questions, collecting and analyzing data, and communicating the data. She noted, however, that there is a need for scaffolding and structure to support students in all of these actions, particularly if the goal is for students to develop data science competencies. Jones agreed and said that citizen science can look very different from place to place, and it is important to pay attention to what types of agency are being prioritized. For example, a project in which students are measuring water pollutants may use methods given to them by a local researcher. In this example, said Jones, disciplinary agency is prioritized. While this is not necessarily a bad thing, it brings up questions of what the students are learning about water sampling, and whether they are understanding the various approaches and why certain methods may be used.

3

Current Landscape of Data Science Education

Not only is it important to have a vision of the goals and intended learning and outcomes for K–12 data science education, but it is also crucial to understand what is happening and how data science is being incorporated into K–12 settings. This chapter summarizes the presentations and discussions from three sessions: one on hearing from practitioners who work in or with schools implementing data science education, one examining the broader contexts in which data science can be situated to offer more meaningful and relevant data science experiences for students, and the last focusing on the integration of data science with other content area.

HEARING FROM PRACTICE

This session explored the reality on the ground in data science education, with a deep focus on the specifics of designing student learning opportunities. Topics included student learning progressions, opportunities for integration between data science and other subjects, and the wraparound resources needed for implementation. The session started with an overview by Zarek Drozda (Data Science 4 Everyone, University of Chicago), session moderator, of a commissioned paper on the national landscape of K–12 data science implementation. Four panelists who work in or with schools in implementing data science education gave brief overviews of their work and then participated in a moderated Q&A.

Overview of Data Science Programs

There has been an explosion of growth in data science programs over the last several years, said Drozda. However, despite this growth, data science education is currently reaching only a small percentage of students. In a paper commissioned for the workshop, Drozda and his colleagues used a variety of methods to survey the landscape of K–12 data science implementation, but he cautioned that the data are incomplete.[1]

Drozda shared a map (Figure 3-1) of the states that had statewide discrete data science education programs as of the summer of 2022; he noted that this map excludes hundreds of individual school and district programs. There are now 14 states with data science programs, compared to only two statewide programs in 2019, he said. Drozda estimated that there are over 1,600 schools or districts with active K–12 data science programs; this translates to over 2,000 teachers reaching over 180,000 students. Proportionally, this means that there are programs at around six percent of high schools, with 0.1 percent of high school teachers and 3.6 percent of high school students participating. He noted that the implementation of data science in K–12 schools is a global phenomenon, with programs in countries including Israel, China, South Korea, Australia, New Zealand, Germany, the United Kingdom, Sweden, and Mexico.

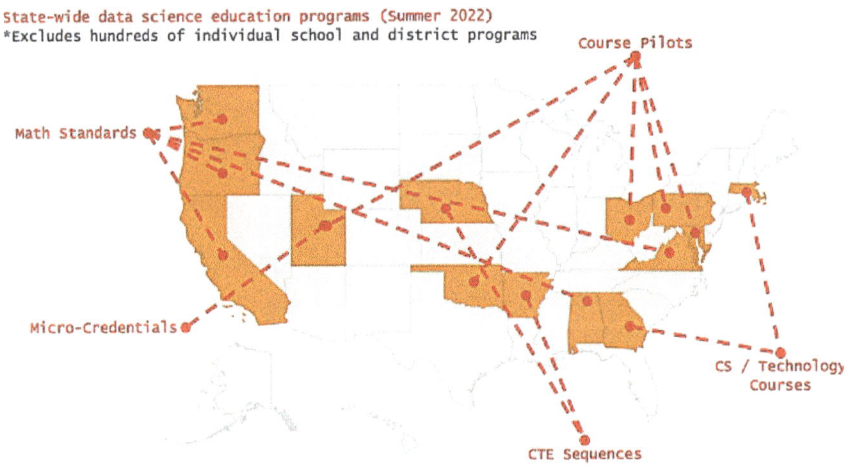

FIGURE 3-1 Discrete data science programs.
SOURCE: Presentation by Zarek Drozda, September 14, 2022.

[1]https://www.nationalacademies.org/event/09-13-2022/docs/D688ED916E82498DA0E2171A109936D679FD5DE26556

Drozda and his colleagues also looked at the frameworks and standards that guide content across school subjects, in order to determine where and to what extent data science is included. A survey of cross-state standards in mathematics, statistics, science, and computer science found 21 shared data-related topics across subjects, as well as multiple meaningful references to data. For example, he said, the College, Career, and Civic Life (C3) Framework for Social Studies State Standards[2] uses the word "data" 53 times. However, Drozda cautioned that these existing guidelines are potentially not enough for data science education.

He and his colleagues also conducted a series of stakeholder interviews across the country to surface the perspectives of teachers. Teachers reported a number of barriers to data science implementation, including:

- Statistics is often cut from algebra courses, or data are brushed over or are secondary to a discipline;
- Low teacher confidence persists in data analysis, technology, or statistical thinking;
- A lack of technology exists;
- A lack of standards or guidance exists around privacy, bias in data sets, data monetization, or other data ethics issues; and
- Methods are too simplistic rather than reflecting the modern world of data and computing.

In statewide K–12 programs, data science content most frequently appears in mathematics classes, followed by career technical education, computer science, science, and social studies (Figure 3-2). Drozda noted that there is a tension between integration and focus; data science reaches more students when it is integrated into existing classes, but it is more likely to be taught with a dedicated focus and fidelity when it is offered as a discrete elective to fewer students. If classes are designed well, however, "you can have the best of both worlds." Drozda gave an example from Oregon, where data science is infused into the core sequence that all students complete in their first two years of high school, and then elective classes are offered to enable some students to focus more deeply. He noted that there is no perfect pathway to teach data science, and that each student and their educational trajectory is individual. Drozda encouraged workshop participants to consider how they can increase options for students and how they can make data science in earlier grades work as a "launchpad" rather than a "filter" to encourage students to move toward data-related pathways.

---

[2]https://www.socialstudies.org/standards/c3

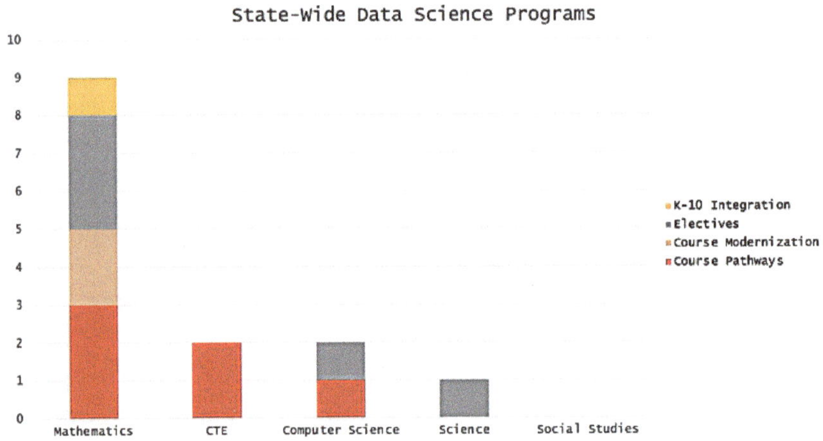

FIGURE 3-2 Frequency of data science programs across subjects in statewide programs.
SOURCE: Presentation by Zarek Drozda, September 14, 2022.

Los Angeles Unified School District, California

In 2010, the Los Angeles Unified School District (LAUSD) and the University of California, Los Angeles (UCLA) were awarded a grant to bring statistical and computational thinking to math, science, and computer science classrooms, said Suyen Machado (UCLA). They began by creating modules to integrate data into algebra, biology, and computer science classes; she said this experience led to three insights. First, it is difficult to compete with established curricula. For example, teachers have a set of standards to meet over the course of the year in Algebra I. Many teachers did not see the connection between data science and the subject of the class, so there was a lot of attrition between summertime professional development and actual implementation. The second lesson was that a six-week module is not enough time to teach the concepts deeply, or for students to get to interact with data as much as they should have. The third lesson, said Machado, was that the program suffered in part because of a lack of awareness about the importance of data science. At the time, it was difficult to even find schools that offered statistics to high school students.

With these lessons in mind, the partners created a high school course that introduced students to dynamic data analysis, tools (R via RStudio class platform), as well as the necessary techniques and principles for reasoning about the world with data. Machado said there was a "perfect storm" of circumstances that allowed the Introduction to Data Science course to take hold. First, the Common Core State Standards were being adopted, which included calls for statistics to be included in high school level algebra and geometry classes. Second, there was a lot of momentum in the computer science area, including new computer science standards and the "computer science for all" movement. This was the "perfect opportunity" to create a course where students could authentically engage with data, and also make the standards for math practice come alive through data. Machado emphasized that although their original intention was to integrate data science into existing courses, their experiences led to the realization that there was a need for a standalone high school data science course. The course was piloted with 10 teachers in LAUSD in 2014 and has now been adopted nationally and internationally.

San Diego Unified School District, California

In 2020, when education was largely remote due to the COVID-19 pandemic, the San Diego Unified School District (SDUSD) began piloting a curriculum called CourseKata,[3] said Stephanie Melville (SDUSD). One of the valuable aspects of CourseKata, she said, is its unique professional development structure. The curriculum includes ongoing professional development for teachers that includes content, pedagogy, workshops, office hours, and collaborative spaces. Melville explained that teachers get an "initial boost" at a study group, and then have ongoing opportunities to learn and share ideas with others. For example, two of the initial adopter educators did not know each other but soon began sharing quizzes, tests, and ideas for projects. This study group now has six teachers in it from four different schools; Melville noted that this type of opportunity to work with others is "kind of a big deal" because schools generally only have one standalone statistics teacher. The group also holds daily Zoom office hours to support teachers who are new to the program. Melville said that teachers participate in the ongoing professional development "even if they don't have to." They go to support each other, to learn different ways of doing things, and to learn how to best support students in their learning.

The plan is to expand data science education into all courses, from pre-K through grade 12, said Melville. However, there are a lot of details to figure out. She compared the K–12 space to a dimly lit room where there are flashlights in cabinets labeled "pedagogy," "methodology," and "curriculum"; everyone is searching for the fix that will make math relevant and meaningful to students. Prior to this program, there was a single track to graduation for math, and many students were opting to not continue to study math. Adding data science to the curriculum in SDUSD has created

---

[3]https://coursekata.org/

an entirely new pathway to graduation, said Melville, and has opened doors for many underserved populations including Black, Latino, and low-income students.

Fairview High School, Colorado

Paul Strode (Fairview High School) teaches high school biology and incorporates data and statistics into every part of the curriculum. His journey to this approach, he explained, began when he was a college student with no real understanding of how to use data. Statistics was not an available class in his high school, and he chose not to take a college statistics class in part because it was five days a week at eight in the morning. As part of his biology degree, he did an independent research project on water quality; he used some statistics in the project but didn't understand what they meant. After graduation, Strode began teaching high school biology, and the only data analysis conducted in his classes was the Chi-square test. He noted this is typical high school biology content, and he "didn't understand even that simple calculation that well." Once Strode began graduate school, he came to the realization that he needed to "pull back the curtain" on data and actually learn how statistics were calculated and what they meant. When he headed back to teaching, he brought this new understanding with him and wanted to convey it to his students. Data science is foundational and constant in his biology class, with students computing descriptive statistics by hand (e.g., *t* test, regression analysis, variance). This approach "has made all the difference" because the students understand the operations and what the data mean. Strode said that teachers sometimes ask him how long his statistics unit is, and he tells them, "There's no unit… It's just seamless. It's part of every single unit that we cover."

Mobile City Science

Katie Headrick Taylor (University of Washington) said that her work with data science programs could be best described as "first doing the work and then naming it much later." She explained that 12 years ago, when her work involved supporting young people to collect data about the lack of transportation in their cities, data science was not a construct that she was aware of. However, the process of collecting data and using those data to make arguments for resources in the community brought up many of the same issues and questions that have been discussed at this workshop, she said. For example, who gets to decide what "counts" as data? Once data are constructed and imbued with epistemic authority, what are the material consequences for people's homes, schools, parks, neighborhoods, and lives? Taylor's project on transportation, now called Mobile City Science,[4] demonstrates the "promise and precarity" of data, the contentious and politically fraught decision-making process, and how wielding data can usurp relations of power. It is still an open question, she said, whether giving data and data practices to young people of color is sufficient support to undo and re-imagine problems that are the products of years of racist and misogynistic systems. Further, does calling this process "data science" move us any closer to that goal?

Moderated Discussion and Audience Q&A

Following the panelists' remarks, Drozda moderated a Q&A session followed by audience Q&A.

Program Design

Drozda asked the panelists to comment on how educators could think about designing their own programs, and to describe what an "exciting, meaningful, and impactful" K–12 data science education experience looks like. Taylor responded that sometimes educators are already doing data science without knowing it. She noted that during the COVID-19 pandemic, nearly everyone was engaged in some form of data literacy, trying to make decisions about where to go and who to see when there were so many unknowns. The pandemic helped us, Taylor explained, to realize the consequentiality of data, and the fact that we need data to make decisions about how to stay safe and healthy. Connecting data to students' everyday lives and facilitating advocacy opportunities can bring data science to life. Taylor's work on Mobile City Science demonstrated how data are necessary for making decisions about the health and well-being of communities and neighborhoods. Young people wanted bike lanes to safely move around the community, so they collected geospatial data of daily routines, highlighted "mobility deserts" and dangerous intersections, and made visualizations to convey their findings. These data, combined with participation in neighborhood planning conversations and other efforts, resulted in a new bike lane that links outdoor areas, the school, and the public library. Taylor noted that there have been mixed results with respect to changes in the community for similar Mobile City Science efforts in other cities; some young people followed a very similar progression of data advocacy but did not achieve concrete changes in their neighborhoods. However, she emphasized that lack of a tangible change does not mean that the process was meaningless

[4] https://www.education.uw.edu/mcs/

to the students, and that learning how to engage with data to advocate for their own neighborhoods is an invaluable educational opportunity.

Strode agreed that hands-on participation by students is essential for quality data science education. He shared several examples of his classroom activities. In his biology classes, students collect data on themselves; for example, students take measurements such as heart rate, arm span, and height, and use apps to visualize the data and determine if and where there are relationships. The students enjoy being able to see their own and their classmates' data points on the screen, he said. Another project involves students collecting data to detect patterns in nature. Students choose a relationship to explore, collect data either systematically or randomly, and then use tools to visualize and analyze the data. For example, one group of students collected data on the height of a plant and the number of branches it had. By collecting 150 data points, they found a "beautiful" exponential relationship between the two measurements. The students, said Strode, realized that they would not have found the relationship with only a few data points, and they were very excited about their findings. Finally, Strode said that he uses published papers to create a dataset, then allows the students to analyze and visualize the data themselves. When they discover that their creations are similar or identical to those in the paper, "that's exciting for them."

Figuring out the story that's in the data is "part of the magic" for students, said Melville. Rather than starting with the data or the calculations, she said she has found the most success when she allows students to "look out into the world" to see what relationships might exist and how they might detect them. Melville said that while practicing calculations is important, it doesn't always bring more students to the table of conceptual understanding; her primary goal is ensuring that data science education is meaningful, impactful, and powerful, particularly for historically excluded populations. Her students often share what they are excited about, and they see math, coding, and data science as tools for figuring the world out. Some students see connections that motivate them to take action—for example, advocating for a crisis hotline phone number on student ID cards to address a lack of mental health services. Melville said that this educational process is "beautiful" to watch, and that her students "love the story so much they don't even realize—maybe they don't even care—that it's hard math they're doing."

Machado described an exciting, meaningful, impactful data science experience as one that engages diverse learners and provides authentic learning experiences. The Introduction to Data Sciences course[5] uses a model of "participatory sensing," in which students use their devices or cell phones to collect data about themselves or anything they're interested

[5]https://www.ucladatascienceed.org/introduction-to-data-science-curriculum

in. She emphasized that students are engaged and interested when the data are personal to them—whether because the data are about them or their interests, or because they are consequential to the students' lives. Data science, said Machado, needs to be focused on the learner. Learners should have the ability to develop the questions that can be answered with data, they should be involved in the collection of the data, and the data should connect to their world. Machado gave the example of high school students posing a question about who is most likely to survive by the end of a horror movie (e.g., certain genders or races). Students can collect their own data, upload them into tools, and analyze the data to find their answers. In closing, Machado shared the "Data Science Sniff Test," as created by Tim Erickson. She noted that there are sometimes questions about the difference between data science and statistics, and that Erickson's description can make it clearer. The Sniff Test describes data science as a situation in which the participant is "doing data moves" and is "awash in data" (i.e., there are so many data, they are messy, and they need to be cleaned up), and the data have certain properties (i.e., are unruly and need to be unpacked), which goes beyond what you might get in a statistics class.

Resources

Drozda asked the panelists to identify the resources that teachers and others need to implement quality data science education. Strode responded that teachers need lots of training. He said that there is "lots of fear" around data, and teachers are asking for help. Machado agreed that training for teachers is critical, noting that teachers come with a wide range of knowledge but sometimes lack the conceptual understanding of data science. She added that another important stakeholder group is high school counselors and administrators. Machado and her colleagues bring these groups together for a professional development session to better understand data science, so that they are able to help students choose their courses and pathways. She noted that administrators also need education about the importance and role of data science because they are "bombarded" with mandates in all subject areas. Melville added that teachers can only do so much to convince students that data science is important and relevant. If counselors or university admissions staff continue to prioritize courses such as calculus over data science, there is a disconnect. She said implementing data science education will require changes in the messaging and actions in higher education. Taylor encouraged workshop participants to think about how to distribute the onus of teaching across a variety of professionals with disciplinary expertise in making sense of data. In addition, she said libraries can be a great resource for students and communities. There is a need for research in this area in order to determine the best models for teaching data science and how to involve people from multiple sectors and disciplines.

Assessments

A virtual workshop participant asked about the role of assessments in data science education. Machado responded that there is a need to come to a consensus about what the learning progression for data science looks like before considering what assessments should look like. However, she emphasized that the conversations should focus on authentic assessment rather than "more multiple-choice tests."

Students' Data

Victor Lee (Stanford University) said that he has been working in the field of data science for many years and has noticed a recent resistance to the idea of classes using data collected from students. Although student-based data are relevant and interesting to students, there are concerns about privacy. He asked panelists to comment, and what they might say to policymakers or teachers about this issue. Taylor said that these concerns are substantiated and well founded, and it is critical to set up agreements with students about how their data will be used and who will be able to access them. For example, data may be anonymized but viewable at the aggregate level. These are thorny ethical issues, she said, and it is essential to communicate about boundaries and to allow students to opt out whenever they are not comfortable. Machado said that early in their Introduction to Data Science course, students collect data using their cell phones. Steps are taken to guard the data, including anonymizing and aggregating them, and giving students some opt out options. Later in the course, students design their own data collection; as teachers, it is our job to guard those data, she said.

Relationship with Other Disciplines

Christine Hirst Bernhardt (Einstein Fellow, University of Maryland) observed that many of the activities discussed at the workshop are already happening in science classrooms (e.g., videos of data visualizations from the National Aeronautics and Space Administration), and wondered whether there are conversations being held about how to strengthen data science education within science courses. Strode responded that although many teachers use visualizations of data to teach, fewer are finding or creating datasets for students to engage with. Some teachers say that there is not enough time for true data science education in their classes, he said, but he has found that incorporating data science throughout the curriculum does not add a significant amount of time. A participant added that teachers from multiple disciplines have complained about the time it takes to teach students how to interpret data and graphs "over and over again"; he noted that making investments upfront in data science education might ultimately save time in the long run.

CONTEXTUAL FACTORS FOR K–12 DATA SCIENCE EDUCATION

Previous speakers have noted that when learning is relevant to youth, they engage more deeply in it and begin to initiate and drive their own learning, said Tammy Clegg (University of Maryland). To create these types of learning opportunities, we need to understand how and in what contexts data science is relevant to learners, she said, as well as what topics they are already interested and engaged in. The goal of this session is to explore the research on the settings and contexts of K–12 data science education with an emphasis on what data science looks like in these contexts and the connections with broader informal contexts that are relevant to K–12 learners' lives. Each panelist in the session made brief remarks about their work, followed by a Q&A session moderated by Clegg.

Online Privacy and Security

"Most of my research is geared at trying to make the Internet a more trustworthy and inclusive space for all kinds of users, including K–12 learners," said Marshini Chetty (University of Chicago). Since 2016, Chetty and her colleagues have been studying how K–5 learners deal with privacy and security concepts in the classroom, at home, and in other environments. The project focuses on issues including data access, data collection, data management, and questions about who collects data and why. Chetty noted that K–5 students generally have little opportunity to learn about data; teachers do not have the training or time to teach these concepts, and parents often defer to teachers on the topic. As a result, she said, these students lack critical data literacy. For example, students in an under-resourced school on the south side of Chicago may not be aware of data being collected on them from neighborhood cameras, or how this collection of data affects them or their communities.

Most efforts to teach children about online privacy and security start around middle school, said Chetty, because this is when children are spending time online and using social media. She compared this practice to "teaching kids how to swim in a pool when it's already full of sharks," and said that starting at a younger age is critical. Building a foundation about data science, privacy, and security as early as kindergarten allows for these concepts to be built upon as children begin to use technologies and the internet.

Leveraging Student Interest: Data Literacy Through the Arts

Kayla DesPortes (New York University) told workshop participants about her work on data literacy through the arts;[6] the project is aimed at exploring the co-design of data art units with middle school art and math teachers to examine how various arts disciplines can couple with data literacy to be mutually supportive. DesPortes works on two different units: data dance and data comics. In the data dance unit, students choose topics they are interested in and analyze data on the topic. For example, a group of students interested in women's rights explored bar graphs that reflected the proportion of respondents who agreed with the statement, "A woman's most important role is to take care of her home and children." The graphs showed how responses differed among geographic regions and between men and women. The students then choreographed a dance, which DesPortes described: "All four dancers are representing females. We start by doing movements lower and work toward higher levels to show women working up toward their goals over time. All dancers then walk in circles to show different roles women can take if the perception is changed like it has been in North America and Latin America." This transdisciplinary practice changed how learners worked across both data science and dance, said DesPortes. Learners practiced embodying numbers and values in dance movements by, for example, exploring the shape of the graph or the numerical values. They embodied the context and implications of the data through an exploration of the variables and how they are situated in the world. Students worked together to make meaning through collaborative movements and practiced interpreting and critiquing dance through perspective-taking as an audience member.

Integrated Computational Thinking

"My work focuses broadly on the intersection between values, social futures, and institutional change in digital learning," said Rafi Santo (Telos Learning). Santo shared his insights into the institutional dynamics related to bringing data science into K–12 settings, based on his experience with the Integrated Computational Thinking project.[7] Through his work on computer science education, Santo and his colleagues found that K–12 administrators were looking to develop K–12 groups and sequences

[6] https://wp.nyu.edu/riddle/projects/building-data-literacy-through-the-arts/
[7] https://ctintegration.org/

around computer science that were district-wide and comprehensive, and that middle school options were quite limited. Computer science tended to be integrated into science and math classes, and when administrators attempted to integrate the subject into other disciplines, "they often found themselves facing a coup." Santo explained that while there is a close relationship between computer science and math and science, teachers in the humanities tended to push back against integrating computing and data into their courses. The goal of the Integrated Computational Thinking program was to identify design principles that would integrate computational thinking into language arts, social studies, and arts while enhancing disciplinary learning in these areas. In addition, Santo and his colleagues wanted to understand the institutional and disciplinary factors that mediate the possibilities for meaningful integration, and to develop evidence-based professional development resources that support computational thinking integration in these subject areas.

Santo highlighted one integration pathway: analyzing texts through computational methods; engaging in data practices for social studies inquiry; and seeing data in art and making data as art. Santo noted that in the course of their research, he and his colleagues identified a number of tensions that speak to the epistemic and cultural differences between computational thinking and the humanities: contextual reductionism, procedural reductionism, epistemic chauvinism, threats to epistemic identities, and epistemic convergence.[8] He highlighted the tension of "epistemic chauvinism," in which computational thinking epistemologies are elevated at the expense of the epistemologies of other subject areas; this can lead to the sidelining of existing ways of knowing, he said. Another tension, said Santo, can occur when learners who identify with humanities-related epistemologies feel alienated by the elevation of computational thinking identities (e.g., an "art kid" resists being asked to do math in art class). Santo emphasized that these theoretical tensions need to be taken seriously when considering whether and how to integrate data science into other subject areas.

[8]*Contextual Reductionism:* valuation of the abstract and quantifiable overrides the valuation of nuance particularly in historical events or literacy texts; *Procedural Reductionism:* inappropriate application of algorithmic logics to knowledge production; *Epistemic Chauvinism:* elevation of computational thinking epistemologies at the expense of those related to a focal discipline leading to "sidelining" existing ways of knowing; *Threats to Epistemic Identities:* elevation of computational thinking identities alienating learners who identify with epistemic identities associated with humanities disciplines; *Epistemic Convergence:* "reskinning" certain humanities practices as computational thinking foreclosing possibilities for substantial interdisciplinary novelty in problem solving. Definitions provided through presentation by Rafi Santo, September 13, 2022.

Data Science for All

Data Science for All is an initiative to identify and address equity, literacy, and data science across sectors, said Stephen Uzzo (New York Hall of Science). The project is part of a regional initiative called Northeast Big Data Innovation Hub,[9] which was created to build a community of practice for cultivating a data-literate society and to establish a baseline set of principles to define what it means to be data literate. Uzzo and his colleagues brought together experts in a process of collaborative inquiry, culminating in a workshop to identify pathways into literacy that could be developed through informal settings such as libraries, cultural institutions, and community centers. They also identified organizational needs, such as the need for resources and training for library staff so they could better serve their patrons.

Uzzo shared the details of one data literacy project that focused on young children. "Big Data for Little Kids" brought together early learners and their families from immigrant and under-resourced communities. Families worked together in a museum to collect data, compile and organize the data, and interpret the data. The study found that families with young children can actively engage in data science, and that parents and children can talk about a wide range of data science concepts, said Uzzo.

Another project brought together educators, designers, learning scientists, and tool developers to identify barriers and opportunities for equitable data science education at the high school level. This convening resulted in several conclusions, said Uzzo, including the need for inclusive tools, resources, and curricula; the need for teacher support and teacher enfranchisement in the process; the need for integrating data science across the curriculum; and the need to make data science available to all students. Based on these findings, Uzzo and his colleagues partnered with STEM Teachers NYC to conduct monthly co-design workshops in which teachers and tool and curriculum developers worked together to identify integration strategies for data science and learning progressions that could be applied to curricula. Each workshop, said Uzzo, functioned like a design charrette—teachers drove the agenda, provided use cases, and focused on integration of data tools and techniques.

In another collaborative project called DataJam, teams of students brainstorm a research question, formulate a hypothesis, use big data to uncover answers, make their own data visualizations, and present their findings. The teams receive assistance and guidance from DataJam mentors. In one example of this project, a team from the Parliament of Mission

[9]https://nebigdatahub.org/

Indians conducted a water testing project and presented their findings in both English and their native language.

Moderated Discussion and Audience Q&A

Clegg moderated a Q&A session with panelists by posing her own questions as well as welcoming questions from workshop participants.

Working with Qualitative and Quantitative Data

Clegg began by asking panelists to comment on how they see students understanding and working with quantitative and qualitative data, and if there are ways that data science education needs to shift to better convey the rich context of data. Uzzo responded that using quantitative and qualitative data together to better understand issues such as climate change is an emerging area that educators need to focus on more in order to give students and community members a better understanding of what data are and how they can be used. Santo noted that the epistemic tensions he mentioned between computer science and the humanities are relevant to this issue. For example, contextual reductionism occurs when there is an overemphasis on quantitative data in the abstract rather than taking a holistic perspective of the context and how data fit in. Santo said that using data tools—such as textual analysis—can help students ask critical questions about the value of data, and to consider when and in what contexts quantitative data are useful. These types of practices can "build the muscle" of students to think critically about the use of data in context. DesPortes said that one benefit of the data dance project is that students get to work with quantitative data in a way in which there is no "wrong answer" and that allows students to reflect their interpretation of data in a creative representation of the context.

Buy-in from Stakeholders

During this session, said Clegg, many different stakeholders were mentioned—teachers, parents, librarians, community members, artists, and others. She asked panelists to comment on how to get buy-in from stakeholders, and how engagement with data science can be done in a way that allows stakeholders to do it "on their own terms and in their own ways." Chetty responded that "buy-in is really tough." Educators have an enormous amount on their plate already and bringing in data science adds to their load. Data science learning needs to be everywhere—from math class to art class—but getting buy-in from teachers will require professional development and resources to give them the confidence and the tools they need to integrate data science into their classes. For example, said Chetty, "micro lessons" can be developed so teachers can easily incorporate a small lesson about data without adding an extra burden. Chetty added that in addition to buy-in from teachers, there is a need to get buy-in from school district officials and administrators to facilitate the implementation and prioritization of data science education in K–12. Santo concurred with Chetty, saying that making changes in the K–12 system requires participation and willingness of people along the entire chain of command. In order to get people on board, Santo said it is critical to take their concerns seriously. He noted that in his work, they start with the assumption that the teachers don't care about computational thinking or data science. "Then it's our job to figure out" how a data science approach can enhance the work of these teachers. He urged stakeholders to pay attention to what people say they care about rather than assuming they will be excited about the "new shiny thing." Getting buy-in is not a transaction; it is a relational process that requires respect for teachers and their ideas and priorities.

Uzzo agreed that respect is critical to buy-in. Teachers "need to be, want to be, and have to be" involved in the development of tools, resources, and curriculum, and they must be viewed as respected experts in their field. Teachers have been enthusiastic participants during the co-design workshops that Uzzo has conducted, and their insight has been essential. For example, at one workshop, tool designers asked the teachers why they weren't using the tools that were available. Teachers responded that one of the tools required a blog, and they weren't allowed to have a blog. People were "gobsmacked," said Uzzo; the tool designers had no idea that this was why tools weren't being used. DesPortes added that stakeholders vary in terms of their ability or support to be co-designers; she stressed the importance of flexibility and building relationships with partners.

Creating a Collaborative Environment

Expanding on the idea of getting buy-in from stakeholders, Clegg asked panelists to comment on how data scientists need to think differently about data science to welcome stakeholders from across multiple disciplines and practices. Santo replied that "enormous amounts of listening" are always the first step to understand the context, the communities, and the concerns of potential partners. Further, he said, we need to be intentional about whose goals are being served and what communities are truly asking for. For example, if a community organization is interested in having a data science program because there are good jobs in that field, it is important to keep this specific end goal in mind when designing a program. He emphasized again that building relationships is critical to success. Uzzo agreed that listening is "job one." Communities and stakeholders have essential questions that they want answered, and data scientists can help facilitate the process of answering them. For example, in his work on hazards in coastal communities, they use participatory modeling[10] to help community members explore scenarios and make decisions about policies and resources that are needed.

Overcoming Math Phobia

A virtual workshop participant noted that "math phobia" is common, even among teachers, and asked how to overcome this barrier to incorporating data science. DesPortes responded that in her work with math and art teachers, each side was "phobic" of the other side's discipline. She said that the teachers didn't necessarily overcome these phobias but instead worked together to put scaffolding in place so that students had the support they needed to work across disciplines. Santo said that he is math phobic, but there are tools that allow him to willingly engage in data science. When there is an "authentic context and relationship to a problem to be solved" combined with useful tools and resources, people are motivated to work and dive into the data. Chetty commented that it could be very helpful for people to see that there are math-phobic data scientists like Santo; she said that "representation matters." Uzzo shared his opinion that math phobia is largely due to the way that math is taught, and there is a need for change in math education. He said that math is often taught first as abstract ideas and equations rather than through the real-world problems that can be solved using math as a tool.

Goal of Data Science Integration

V. Lee reflected on the discussions about integrating data science into other disciplines and said he had heard three different potential goals or approaches for this work. First, he said, other disciplines can be seen as a "Trojan horse" that is used to get students to engage with data and become data literate. In this goal, data are the point. A second approach is to use data to improve students' understanding of and engagement with the other disciplines; here, data are subservient. Finally, there is a third approach where data open up opportunities for new forms of expression and exploration. Clegg added that she thinks the third approach is the right one, with the ultimate goal of educating students to be literate participants in an increasingly connected world.

---

[10]In this approach, "participants co-formulate the problem and use modeling practices to aid in the description, solution, and decision-making actions of the group" (https://participatorymodeling.org/).

INTEGRATION INTO OTHER CONTENT AREAS

This session explored the ways in which data science has been integrated with other subjects beyond mathematics. Panelists shared details of their own work and discussed various approaches for integrating data science into the study of other content areas in both school-based and out-of-school contexts. Camillia Matuk (New York University) moderated the session. Each of the five panelists described their approach to data science, followed by a Q&A session.

Four Key Elements to Data Science Integration

Emmanuel Schanzer (Bootstrap) introduced himself as a proud former public school math teacher, computer scientist, and co-founder of an organization called Bootstrap.[11] Bootstrap reaches more than 30,000 students each year in 49 states, in grades 5–12. The program works to integrate data science into mathematics, physics, history and social studies, and life/Earth sciences. As a curriculum architect, Schanzer said he thinks of curriculum design like baking a cupcake. There is room for flexibility, but there are also certain ingredients that are essential to a cupcake. At Bootstrap, there are four ingredients that are considered key to data science education: statistics, computing, civic responsibility, and domain investment. Civic responsibility is necessary in order to put data and analysis in context. For example, using a random sample that is drawn from a "society filled with bias" will result in racially biased algorithms and weaponized social media. It should not solely be on the shoulders of math and computer science teachers to teach this concept (i.e., civic responsibility) to students, nor are they necessarily the best ones to do it. Data science can benefit from the expertise of teachers in other areas—such as history and social studies—and these teachers can benefit from data science.

Domain investment, Schanzer explained, reflects the idea that data science teachers need to be able to go deep in multiple different domains to provide students multiple on-ramps for interest. For example, teaching data science using a dataset about wines in Tuscany versus a dataset about stop and frisk policies is going to have profoundly different impacts on relevance and engagement for students. Data science education can and should draw on diverse datasets, such as climate data, data on COVID-19, and data on gerrymandering. Schanzer said that people who are "scratching their heads" trying to figure out how to integrate data science with non-STEM classes are focusing too heavily on the first two ingredients of data science education (statistics and computing) and not enough on the second two (civic

[11]https://getbootstrap.com/

responsibility and domain investment). Integration works when all four ingredients are valued. For example, he said, instead of trying to convince history teachers to make room for linear regression, we should be thinking about how data on redlining serve the existing goals of that classroom.

Justice-focused Data Science

Angela Calabrese Barton (University of Michigan) studies engagement with data in middle school science, most recently in the context of COVID-19 and sustainable communities. Calabrese Barton shared quotes from students talking about the pandemic to set the stage:

- "I don't see myself in the data."
- "It's not numbers that will solve the pandemic but the stories people tell with numbers... If we don't have different perspectives on the numbers, it will only offer one story. That won't help everyone."
- "It's never only about COVID-19."

Calabrese Barton explained that viewing the pandemic as a socio-scientific issue makes visible how lives are rendered through data, quantifying and categorizing people in communities. In data science education, Calabrese Barton draws upon a data justice framework to explore how and why youth engage with data to make sense of, to make decisions about, and to take action on science-related issues. She shared three key takeaways from this justice-based framework. First, "datafication" does not impact all people equally. Data science education should consider the ways in which engaging with data takes place in socio-historical and political contexts, shaping what and whose data are made accessible and visible. Second, learning and engaging with and about data involves more than cognitive processes. Students also employ senses and feelings, and tools need to be developed to support youth in using these senses and feelings in making sense of data and taking action toward meaningful social change, she said. Third, data science involves epistemic (in)justice; that is, data are always produced and engaged from multiple epistemic positions, and how such productions are recognized as legitimate forms of knowing and doing in science matters. This has implications not only for what is taught, said Calabrese Barton, but also how it is taught and how it is assessed.

Enacting data justice in learning environments requires attention to how young people engage with and use data toward affecting their own and others' lives, social relations, and possibilities, said Calabrese Barton. She gave several examples of young people's engagement with data. One student, a 12-year-old named Prez, was experiencing mental anguish about COVID-19 in May 2020, in large part because of the data he found on the

Centers for Disease Control and Prevention website about hospitalization and death rates in the Black community. He found that his anxiety was lessened when he watched YouTube videos that encouraged taking reasonable precautions and put the dangers of COVID-19 into context. Calabrese Barton described this process as Prez "producing critical data practices overlaying YouTube with the big data to critique power structures that determine what data and data narratives count, to care for himself when data, society, and science [were] not." As a Black youth, Prez encountered dominant data narratives that invoked harmful racialization and he used critical data practices to move beyond critique toward liberatory outcomes.

Another example that Calabrese Barton shared was of a 15-year-old Black girl named Jasmine who curated a complex data infrastructure involving data from different sources and epistemological origins in order to decide how to safely participate in protests for racial justice. Jasmine researched modes of viral transmission, examined protest images online to analyze mask-wearing and social distancing practices among these groups, and looked at rates and patterns of infection and spread in her city. Jasmine stated, "I had to decide whether to protect myself and my family against injustice by protesting, or to protect myself and my family by not going." Jasmine's journey, said Calabrese Barton, reflected a complex analytic process of weighing different data inputs to mitigate health risks and to fight for justice.

Expanded Approaches to Data

Rahul Bhargava (Northeastern University) asked, "Is it a necessity that working with data requires us to use computational methods and means?" Bhargava said his work tries to demonstrate that the answer is no. He noted that the history of data is rooted in collecting data about the "other" from a position of power and privilege, and doing something different can be a "radical act." For example, he works with community groups to look at data about the community, to produce data when there are gaps, and to find a story in the data to paint as a community mural. Practices like data murals are a way of restating what data are, who they are for, and why they are used, said Bhargava. As data become more central to civic and community decision-making, it is essential that we broaden the people who are invited to the table. This broadened approach can take numerous forms, including building critical data practices, embracing epistemological pluralism, using arts-based approaches, and considering social impact. Bhargava recalled the earlier workshop discussion about math phobia and said that reframing data and data practices is a way to invite all people to the table, regardless of their comfort with math.

Data as Narration of Worlds

Josh Radinsky (University of Illinois at Chicago) works on data science in three areas, all of which inform each other. First, he works in the classroom to create and improve curriculum and instruction. Second, Radinsky studies how people narrate their social worlds using data, texts, and tools. Third, he is engaged in the ongoing struggle for educational justice in Chicago, using data. He described each of these projects in turn. Radinsky has been working in the classroom for 25 years, mostly middle school through college. He works closely with teachers to design and explore ways of introducing data science to students. For example, a tool called Social Explorer[12] allows students to work with Census data from 1790 to the present; Radinsky noted that the excitement of learning with Census data can overcome the barrier of math phobia for many teachers.

Radinsky shared some maps with workshop participants to illuminate how people use data to construct the meaning of themselves, their communities, and their cities. One map demonstrated the disappearance of the middle class in Chicago between 1970 and 2015; another showed the huge racial disparities in police killings in Chicago. These types of data come together to construct the story of Chicago and to reveal how Chicago is different for people of different backgrounds. Radinsky said that data science education should reflect this approach of using data to construct meaning for our everyday lives.

His third area of work involves using data to advocate for educational justice in Chicago. Some city projects have devastated public schools but at the same time sparked "incredible organizing" of parents, community groups, and others who are fighting in support of public schools. Data are a powerful tool in this debate, he said, and they are used by both sides to make their arguments. Overarching all of these projects, said Radinsky, is the idea that data, texts, and tools are central to how we learn about the social world and change it. He emphasized that narrating data should be understood as a way we engage with and change the world, not just a secret code for describing it. Data science education needs to teach about data as part of—not separate from—our human relationships.

Data in a Youth Newsroom

Lissa Soep (Vox Media, LLC) spoke with workshop participants about her work at YR Media (formerly Youth Radio). YR Media is a platform and learning center for emerging digital media creators to report on and produce stories about pressing social issues. Headquartered in Oakland, YR

[12]https://www.socialexplorer.com/

Media works with young people from across the country; most collaborators are youth of color and youth who have been ignored or betrayed by society. YR Media's focus on arts and music is vital to how it uses data to produce stories, said Soep, noting that she comes from a humanities background and is "not a data nerd." To her, the integration of data into journalism is a recognition that data are needed to move the conversation in the direction that young people are organizing for.

Soep shared several examples of the work being conducted at YR Media. The first example was a project called "Can You Teach AI to Dance?" This project, she said, stemmed from a discovery that Spotify uses a hidden, artificial intelligence (AI)-based rating system that scores songs on the basis of a number of qualities, including danceability. "These were fighting words" for the young people, who did not want to be told by AI which songs were danceable. They developed an interactive experience that invites users to compare their ratings against the AI ratings; in the process, the project reveals and unpacks how AI is operating in this space and what type of data are being used. The second example was called "Erase Your Face." This project explored facial recognition tools by inviting users to digitally scribble over a face in order to determine how difficult it is to go undetected. The third project was "Surveillance U," part of a year-long investigation into virtual proctoring tools[13] that are becoming more commonly used, particularly during the pandemic. Soep said that this project was spurred by nearly 90 petitions filed by students to stop the use of these tools; students' concerns included mental health impacts, harms to the learning environment, and privacy and bias issues.

There are several frameworks that are relevant to this work, said Soep. The first is a framework she has developed with a colleague for critical data expression (or critical computational expression; Figure 3-3). Critical data expression, which is at the intersection of technology, justice, and art, involves using data as storytelling material, and discovering, analyzing, and sharing data in expansive ways that engage young people and people in positions of power to bring change.

Another key framework, said Soep, is "humanizing collegial pedagogy," which requires rich collaborations between young people and veterans; through these collaborations, humanity is made central in an effort to hold young people accountable to themselves, their peers, their partners, and to the broader public. Digital afterlife is another framework that accounts for what the work will do once it is released into the world, said Soep. Unlike a traditional classroom assignment that is turned in to the teacher, the work

[13]A simulator that is given to users to experience what it's like to have your every move monitored under the suspicion that you may or may not be cheating on tests that are being taken remotely.

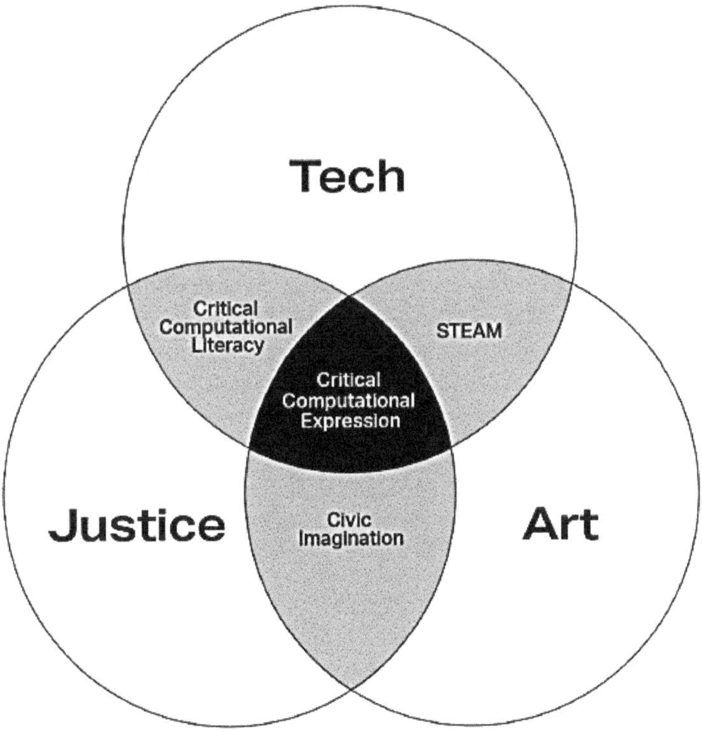

FIGURE 3-3 Critical computational expression.
SOURCE: Adapted from Lee and Soep, 2023.

done at YR Media is published and becomes part of the national conversation. This requires a framework like digital afterlife that centers not only on findings but moves forward toward dialogue and engagement.

In closing, Soep shared a quote from an upcoming publication by herself and a colleague: "Through the digital media products they create, young people can reimagine what's possible in their lives and futures, and work with others to pursue that vision for change. Critical [Data] Expression synthesizes vibrant traditions from cultural studies, STEM, and the arts, honoring the interdisciplinarity and deep humanity of a society that depends on, but cannot be reduced to, its near-constant use of technology." (Lee and Soep, 2023).

Moderated Discussion and Audience Q&A

Following the panelists' remarks, Matuk led a Q&A session with panelists and workshop participants.

Looking at Sensitive Issues Through a Data Lens

Matuk began by recalling a comment in Louie's presentation (Chapter 2) about how there is a risk to vulnerable students when teachers aren't prepared to address social and political issues with awareness and sensitivity. She asked panelists to comment on what lessons they have learned through their work about how to best approach socially and politically sensitive issues through a data lens. Schanzer responded that at the same time that he and his colleagues were working in New York City to implement data science education, there was a separate effort to help teachers engage in difficult conversations with students. Some teachers felt as though they'd "been thrown off a cliff," he said, but they found that data science actually could provide a useful framework for these conversations. Schanzer explained that difficult conversations often evoke a strong emotional response, and data can help ground the conversation in facts. Calabrese Barton added her perspective that it is critical to question what is considered productive, legitimate conversation around tensions. She explained that youth are experts of their lives and stories, and the tensions reflected in difficult conversations are not abstract but are grounded in the lives of real people. When teachers introduce difficult topics, it is essential that the conversation reflects the students' lived experiences and the complex and multilayered nature of the topics. Radinsky observed that the concept of "difficult conversations" can mean different things to different people, and conversations can be difficult for both White teachers and non-White teachers. He said that when teachers aim to avoid difficult conversations by, for example, avoiding the topic of race, this makes "all kinds of conversations difficult." He observed that one way of avoiding difficult conversations is by using code words such as "diversity" rather than clearly communicating the name of the racial, ethnic, or other group (e.g., calling a 98% Black school "diverse"). By naming race or other issues clearly and explicitly, we can better see and reach the learning objectives. Bhargava agreed with Radinsky's perspective and said, "If we can't say the word Black...we can't talk about these issues."

Bhargava added that when taking risks in the classroom, he likes to use the analogy of building a playground. On a playground, students might be willing to take risks they wouldn't normally take, willing to swing higher or jump farther. Similarly, if the right environment is present in an educational setting, students may be willing to take risks and have conversations that they are otherwise reluctant to have. For example, he said, he has been working on an approach to data theater that builds on the populist tradition of participatory theater. One of the findings from this work is that people are more willing to question the epistemic power of data in the theater setting than in other more traditional data science settings. The media that we use to examine and explore issues, he said, shape the environment and the conversations that can be held. Soep shared her perspective on difficult topics and difficult conversations, saying that we often lean too quickly toward technology solutions, but it is important to be flexible when leaning into sensitive, emotional, personal, and cultural issues. She shared the example of a story on AI tools that were being used to reanimate still photographs of people who had died; as the reporter was investigating, the story turned away from the details of the technology and more toward an exploration of grief and societal support for those who are grieving.

Applying Lessons to K–12 Classrooms

Given the broad range of experiences discussed in this session, Matuk asked panelists to consider what they had learned from their work that could be applied to data science education in the K–12 system. Specifically, she said, where are opportunities to build on synergies between disciplines and stakeholders?

Calabrese Barton began by emphasizing the importance of considering "who benefits and who gets hurt and what that means for who's at the table" when designing and implementing data science projects. Calabrese Barton and her colleagues have used a co-design approach that gives youth, families, and communities the chance to decide when, how, and why data are produced. Co-design is not something that happens overnight, she said, but instead requires intentional, relational practices and vulnerability. She shared an example of an engineering project that started with two years of work co-designing materials and tools using a data justice lens in community contexts, and then moved into a classroom setting in the third year. Setting this work in the community allowed youth and families to have different forms of authority than they might have if it took place in schools, she said. One of the insights that grew out of the project was a framework called "pedagogies of community ethnography"; this framework centers community knowledge as a valuable part of STEM knowing, creates spaces for co-generating and integrating community knowledge into STEM learning, and provides tools for navigating data from different epistemological origins. This approach, said Calabrese Barton, supports youth in making meaning and engaging in critique and liberatory goals. As youth consider technical specifications for how an engineering design might work, they learn to balance these with the needs and wants of their communities that they have collected through surveys, interviews, and observations. For example, one unit challenged students to develop a prototype that involved multiple energy transformations and a renewable energy source. One group designed a light-up limbo stick in response to their ethnographic findings that "lack of fun" was a big concern among youth in the community. The students, said Calabrese Barton, developed a nuanced and critical view of what "lack of fun" meant for youth; for example, they observed that kids who are bored often get in trouble and lose future opportunities for fun. Calabrese Barton said that this project gave the students the opportunity to both make meaning with and embody the data.

Bhargava shared a story about a fellow teacher's experience with teaching data science in a high school math class. Students were given the assignment of collecting and producing data about an issue they were passionate about, and then giving a presentation on their findings. Students were given multiple options for how to present, including making data sculptures. One student, a Black girl whose mother was facing breast cancer, chose to explore data on breast cancer and the disparate outcomes for women of color. She created a three-dimensional sculpture with two breasts that represented women of color and other women; each breast was layered based on the frequency of incidents or positive outcomes. The sculpture, said Bhargava, communicated data on multiple levels; it spoke to the actual physical condition, the disparities, and the idea of mastectomy. The student won the "students' choice award" for the sculpture; Bhargava noted that the student had not previously been creating work of this quality. This story, he said, speaks to the power of "finding windows and opportunities" to be creative and to challenge students in new ways.

How to Work with NGSS Standards

Andee Rubin (TERC) said that if a science teacher is following the Next Generation Science Standards (NGSS), there is a tension between fidelity to the standards and allowing students to be creative with using their own data. For example, she said, a unit might be designed around students finding specific patterns in a dataset, which requires the teacher to provide data that are specifically curated for this purpose. She asked panelists to comment on this tension and how to balance the needs of student-led data science and NGSS requirements. Radinsky replied that using student-generated data is not always appropriate or ideal, and he often tinkers with datasets to make them work for a particular activity. Mapping to the standards is critical for science classes, he said, and it is possible to get students engaged in datasets that are designed for that purpose by considering "where are the hooks in this dataset?" Getting students engaged and interested is more a matter of the "culture of the classroom," he said, than the particular dataset. Schanzer acknowledged that this tension is real and said that different learning goals require different ways of approaching data science. He agreed with Radinsky that looking for a "hook" in the data is essential and said that there is a need for datasets that have depth and allow students to explore the mysteries within them.

Scalability

Erika Shugart (National Science Teaching Association) observed that many of the projects discussed in this session were "one-offs" that require a very well-prepared teacher. She asked panelists how these types of data science activities could be scaled for implementation into classrooms. Bhargava began by noting that the Data Culture Project[14] website has a suite of 12 activities with curricular guides for teachers; the activities are small and easy to weave into the work of the classroom. Radinsky said that clarity of learning objectives and clarity of assessments are essential for teachers when they are implementing new materials. A site like Social Explorer is useful because it has prepackaged vignettes, but the lack of teaching supports makes it hard for teachers to use. Teachers talking to teachers is the only way that data science innovations will make it into the classroom, he said; teachers need to see examples of how other teachers have made it work.

---

[14]https://databasic.io/en/culture/

4

Supporting Implementation: Tools, Resources, and Teacher Preparation

To implement high-quality data science education in K–12, tools, resources, and teacher training will be needed. This chapter summarizes the presentations and discussions from two sessions, one on tools and resources, and one on teacher preparation.

TOOLS AND RESOURCES

This workshop session explored the tools and data sets that currently exist or that are needed to support data science learning in K–12 education. Tim Erickson (Epistemological Engineering) moderated the session by posing questions to the panelists, followed by a Q&A discussion with workshop participants.

Unplugged Data Science Learning

When we think about tools for data science education, said Erickson, we usually think about computational tools and computer programs. However, there are also offline tools that can be a useful entry point into data science; Erickson asked panelists to describe their experience with unplugged data science learning. Rolf Biehler (Paderborn University, Germany) shared his experience with the use of data cards in primary and middle school classrooms. Data cards, he explained, are cards that each represent an object and have a list of variables and their values for that object (see Figure 4-1). Students can use these cards as data representations to group, separate, and rearrange data, and these physical operations can be transferred

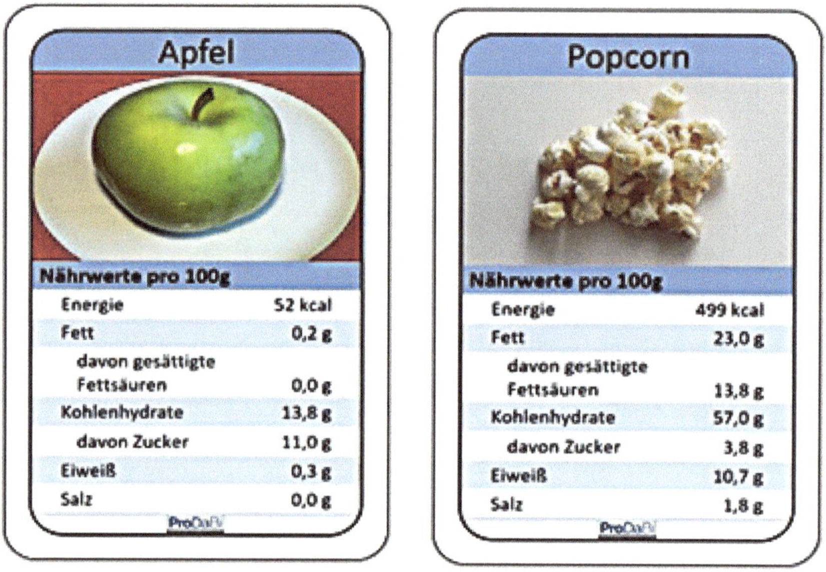

FIGURE 4-1 Two data cards with labels.
SOURCE: Presentation by Rolf Biehler, September 13, 2022. See also www.prodabi.de/en and Podworny et al., 2021.

to digital operations, in particular in the software TinkerPlots.[1] One use for these cards is to introduce students to decision trees as a machine learning method; this topic is part of the required curriculum in fifth and sixth grade in some states in Germany. Biehler described how the cards are used. There are around 50 cards that each represent a food; the cards contain nutritional information such as calories, fat, and sugar per 100g. Students label the cards with colored paper clips to represent whether the food is rather recommendable (green) or rather not recommendable (red) by using the values of the variables on the cards. Students then sort, separate, or stack the cards by various criteria and see the patterns that develop. This is done for data analysis and visualization purposes. What is a new use is that they can be used to create decision trees. For example, a two-step decision tree could be made that sorts the foods first by fat content and then by sugar content (Figure 4-2). The students decide which splits have a low number of misclassifications. This activity is used as a jumping-off point for a discussion about how machines would construct decision trees automatically, said Bieher, by systematically checking which data splits have the lowest number of misclassifications.

[1]https://www.tinkerplots.com/

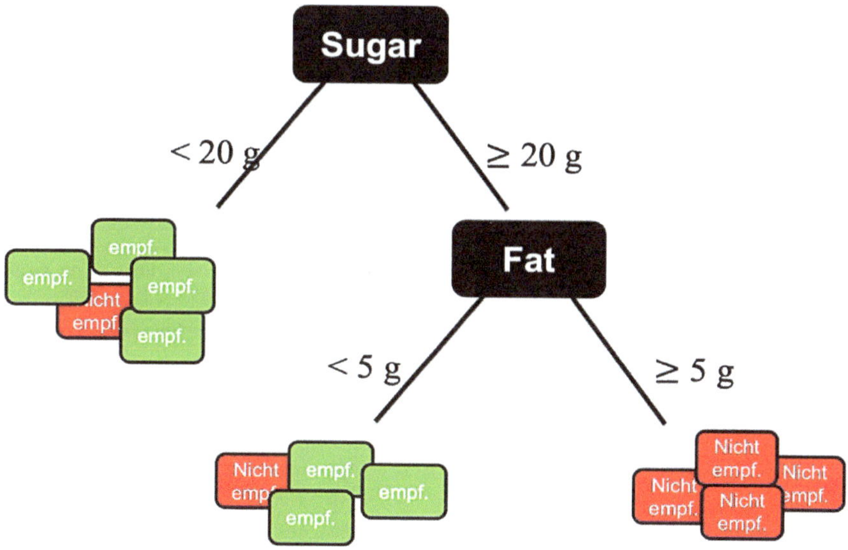

FIGURE 4-2 Two-step decision tree using data cards.
NOTE: "< 20 g" means less than 20 g per 100 g food. Rather recommendable: "empf."; rather not recommendable: "Nicht empf." The classification is done by a majority vote in each subgroup. In this case two items out of 13 will be misclassified.
SOURCE: Presentation by Rolf Biehler, September 13, 2022. See also www.prodabi.de/en and Podworny et al., 2021.

V. Lee said that unplugged data science learning can be done even without specialized materials like data cards. Teachers already have tools—such as Post-it Notes, magnets, and whiteboards—that can be used for data visualizations. These low-tech tools present a rich opportunity to talk about computational thinking and algorithms through discussions of where the next data point should go, what choices are being made, and how different choices result in a different visualization. There are a lot of accessible tools that facilitate powerful learning without the need for expensive technology, said V. Lee. Rubin added that another low-tech option for data visualization is using participants' bodies; for example, participants can make a "graph" by lining up their bodies according to different variables. These visualizations can be mirrored in programs like TinkerPlots or the Common Online Data Analysis Platform (CODAP),[2] she said, making for a clear demonstration of the relationship between analog and digital data analysis. V. Lee said that when teachers are asked what technology they are most inclined to use when discussing data in the classroom, they generally are most comfortable

[2]https://codap.concord.org/

with spreadsheet programs. There is a need to advocate for the use of other visual tools such as CODAP and TinkerPlots, he said, but also important to consider how to meet teachers where they are most comfortable and with the tools they have in front of them.

Common Data Analysis Tools

Erickson asked panelists to comment on their use of common data analysis tools in the classroom, and the capabilities and challenges of each.

R and RStudio

Programming is a big part of how we engage with data science right now, said V. Lee, and the programming language R and the integrated development environment RStudio are used by professional scientists, analysts, and industry. However, R can be a "little unwieldy for newcomers," and may require installations that are complicated for school district IT. V. Lee said it is important to consider when and why programming is necessary, and how it might support learning or create a hindrance. At the same time, he said, students shouldn't be graduating without preparation and experience with tools that are common in the workplace.

Python and Jupyter Notebook

For many computer science educators, said Biehler, R is not an acceptable tool for the classroom; they are looking for programming languages that fit into their world. Python is well received as an attractive programming language that is accessible and interactive, and German computer science programs use Python, along with Jupyter Notebooks, at various levels. In the most elementary level, students use Jupyter Notebooks in a "manual-driven system" that allows for the manual manipulation of certain graphs; Biehler said this is the easiest entrance point. As students advance, educators open cells to show the code and use it to introduce students to simple coding for graphs.

CODAP

Our computer science education always begins with CODAP, said Biehler, which can be used to introduce data exploration in a simple way. Rubin said that CODAP is a "perfect tool" for her work because in short-term courses or out-of-school contexts, it allows students to get up and running with data science. CODAP is web-based, free, and open source, as well as allows drag and drop direct access with "really wonderful" visualization capabilities. Randy Kochevar (Education Development Center) said he is a "huge fan" of CODAP because it was designed from the ground up as an instructional tool. CODAP gives users a "tangible relationship" with the data, facilitates an understanding of the relationship between "case values and data populations," and allows users to look at trends in a way that is simple and user-friendly. Kochevar said that he has used CODAP with students as young as fifth grade to visualize Earth science data or biology data. Rubin cautioned, however, that CODAP is not a perfect tool for all uses; for example, reproducibility, generalizability, being able to use something over with a new set of data are really hard to do in CODAP.

Fathom and TinkerPlots

Fathom and TinkerPlots are two other software packages for data exploration, said Chad Dorsey (Concord Consortium). Fathom is appropriate for high schoolers, whereas TinkerPlots is designed for middle school and younger students.

Progression of Tools

Several speakers have alluded to a progression from simple, web-based tools like CODAP to more programming-oriented software, said Erickson; he asked Dorsey to comment on how this progression works. Dorsey explained that the process starts with a fundamental concept that "a data point is a thing." Data might be viewed in different ways, but the data point never changes or disappears. By foregrounding this concept, students gain the ability to engage with and understand data. Learning tools like CODAP are designed intentionally to highlight these fundamental aspects of data and habits of mind that are necessary for data science education, said Dorsey. The other important component of early data science education, he said, is an "intentional little bit of delight" that entices students to start exploring, to find insights, and to realize that there are multiple insights to be found in data.

Rubin said that progression in data science tools is a research area that is understudied; important questions that need to be answered include the following:

- What does the progression of tools look like?
- How can we help students move from a tool like CODAP to one like R or Python?
- What are the critical changes in the way students think about data or the new skills that they need in order to make the transition?

Considerations for Younger Students

If data science is to be implemented all along the K–12 continuum, said Erickson, there is a need for attention to the younger grades. Kochevar shared his experience working with younger students, saying that developing the habits of mind and fundamental concepts of data at younger ages will facilitate greater gains down the road. However, he noted that there are important considerations when teaching younger students and limits to what can be covered. He gave the example of a project for fourth and fifth graders that used data on rainfall and stream flow. He and his colleagues had their plans reviewed by a teacher, who pointed out that these students hadn't yet covered decimals. One of the challenges in younger grades is remembering where students are and what they have been exposed to previously, said Kochevar. It is important to work closely with educators in order to make sure that the material is appropriate and relevant. Another challenge, he said, is that K–12 educators do not have much personal experience working with data and doing scientific research. There is a need to meet teachers where they are and provide professional development so that teachers can gain the knowledge, experience, and comfort that they need. Dorsey went on to say that there is a tension between using more professional tools and more accessible tools. If data science education is not accessible to people—either teachers or students—it will put people "off right from the get-go." Students who succeed with less accessible tools will succeed no matter what, he said, but it is critical to draw all students in with easy-to-use tools that get them "excited about data."

Diversity, Equity, and Inclusion

V. Lee observed that nearly all of the tools discussed during this session are visualization-intensive and assume a very particular ability. "It behooves us to explore a whole range of ways of data expression using sound, texture, human body," and other ways to explore data that are not solely visual. Unique approaches like the Dance Data project shared by DesPortes (Chapter 3) are critical for bringing all students into data science, regardless of abilities. Students also vary in terms of their backgrounds, interests, and goals, said V. Lee. It is important to consider how data science education is being connected to the specific technologies that students already are interested in—for example, using TikTok videos as data. While some students want to focus narrowly on traditional data science areas or want to learn to program, all students should get a broad view of all of the tools and opportunities that exist.

Datasets

What does it mean to have an appropriate dataset for students? Rubin said that she likes to use the Goldilocks analogy. Many of the datasets that have been used until recently are like the small chair: they are accessible but small and boring. Large datasets are rich with data but are so complicated that students can get lost in them. Our goal, said Rubin, is to find datasets like the middle chair: just right for the purpose and the user. She shared the criteria that she considers when trying to find the right dataset. First, the number of variables matters. Sometimes this decision is made by the tools that we use, but in general Rubin said that she finds that "a screen's worth" is the right number of variables because it allows for easily visualization and manipulation. Rubin said that the number of cases is less important than whether students understand the definition of the variables and cases and can relate to possible relationships among variables. A second criterion is whether a dataset has "something there for them to discover"—that is, whether there are interesting patterns or relationships that students can investigate. A third consideration, she said, is whether the format of the dataset is appropriate for the analysis; she gave an example of a wide format compared to a long format for data on three species of shrimp in several pools in the Puerto Rican rainforest and said that in one case it is easy to compare across species and in another format it is not. This issue was discovered through trial-and-error: students were given the datasets and asked to answer questions that were difficult to investigate the way the data were formatted. V. Lee said that another consideration for datasets is whether they are "too tidy and too clean." Although datasets may require cleaning and simplifying to be usable, students need to be prepared to look at data that are messy. Finding datasets that work for teachers is hard, he said, and is an area that is ripe for progress. Teachers need access to "abundant and continually replenishing datasets that are good for pedagogical purposes."

Wraparound Needs

Erickson asked Kochevar to discuss the need for wraparound resources that help teachers and students use data science tools. Kochevar said that he began teaching in January 2020, which meant that within a few months, he needed to be able to teach everything remotely and sometimes asynchronously because of the COVID-19 pandemic. To do so, he needed more resources than just the data science tool. He needed a place where students could find the instruction set and could record their work and turn it in, and where he could review the work, evaluate it, and give feedback. As wonderful as these tools are, said Kochevar, there is a need for them to be surrounded by resources and other tools that support student learning and teacher instruction. There have been efforts made in these areas, but there is a need for further work to develop wraparound resources that are engaging and accessible.

New Tools

Erickson asked panelists what new tool, or new feature of an existing tool, they would like to see in the future. Biehler responded that he would be happy if CODAP could do everything that Fathom can do. Fathom, he explained, supports data exploration as well as activities such as simulation, understanding probability, randomization, and resampling. He said it is important to be able to combine probabilistic simulation with data exploration. Rubin responded that she would be happy if CODAP could do everything that TinkerPlots does, in particularly segmenting distributions with movable lines. Dorsey stated that he would like a tool that can do things that CODAP, Fathom, and TinkerPlots cannot yet do; specifically, there is a need for tools that can deal with spatio-temporal data. This is a burgeoning area for industry and science, and students need to be prepared.

Audience Q&A

Erickson moderated a Q&A session, taking questions from both in-person and virtual workshop participants.

Selection of Tools

Hollylynne Lee (North Carolina State University) asked panelists about selecting tools for various data science education purposes. Specifically, she wondered what characteristics of tools were useful in forming good data habits and good data practices. V. Lee responded that there is a need to think carefully about how different data science tools connect to the kinds of evidence-based discourse in particular fields. For example, one field may value novel visualizations, so it is important to pick a tool that is well suited for that. Another discipline may require quantitative summaries, and other tools may be more appropriate. Tools should be selected according to how well they fit the norms and style of the discipline in which they will be used. Kochevar added that it is key to be explicit about learning objectives, and tools should be chosen that will allow students to focus on those objectives; "don't put barriers in the way of them doing the thing that you want to have them do," he said. Biehler agreed and noted that students and teachers often need case studies to demonstrate how to use a tool for a certain type of data exploration. In addition, students need worked examples to scaffold, for example, a visualization that they can edit, change, and adapt to their own dataset.

Drozda added to the discussion by noting that there are other tools that have not been mentioned at the workshop, including SAS, Tableau, Stata, Sequel, DataClassroom, and Deepnote. He encouraged educational researchers to look into paid tools that might bring value, as well as ways to make paid tools more affordable for K–12 settings.

Disability Inclusion

Davis Johnstone (Data Science 4 Everyone) said that there has not been enough conversation about disability inclusion in data science, particularly in the area of tools. Current tools often use accommodations that do not work well (e.g., screen readers in coding platforms). Dorsey agreed that this is a major challenge and said that while there are people making an effort in this area, it is a complex and difficult issue to solve. In addition, there is a lack of funding, research, and incentives to make progress. Erickson noted that Tuva has been making strides in accessibility, and Rubin added that several researchers are working on data sonification.

Data Literacy to Data Science Spectrum

Much of the discussion in this session has been focused on tools for data science such as investigation of individual data points, graphing, and other technical practices, observed DesPortes. However, in the real world, the focus is more on data literacy—skills and understandings that are applied in everyday life—rather than data science. For example, when people gather information from news sources, they are selecting data sources, deciding what sources to trust, building arguments based on curated data, and making decisions. She asked panelists if there are tools that can help students develop these types of data literacy skills, or if there are innovations being made in this area. Dorsey agreed that data literacy is essential and argued that data literacy cannot be separated from data science; data exploration is a key part of developing these skills and understandings. Biehler gave an example from Germany, in which students discussed news stories about the gender pay gap and then were given the data to explore themselves. The combination of reading the news and exploring the data, he said, gave them a very different view of the news and how the data were transformed into the stories. Rebecca Nugent (Carnegie Mellon University) agreed with DesPortes that we need more tools and resources to support data literacy, and that it is critical to teach both data literacy and data science. She noted that some students "are incredible technical coders and can't explain anything to anyone."

TEACHER PREPARATION

The role of teachers has been discussed throughout this workshop, said H. Lee. This session was designed to focus on teachers and their preparation to teach data science. Panelists described the current status of preparation, the skills and knowledge that teachers need to have, and ways to incorporate data science into teacher education and professional learning. H. Lee asked the panelists a series of questions, then moderated a discussion with workshop participants.

Current State of Teacher Preparation

What do teachers already know about data science education, asked H. Lee, and how did they develop their knowledge, skills, and dispositions? Stephanie Casey (Eastern Michigan University) responded that teachers believe in making learning experiences meaningful for students, and they can see that incorporating data investigations about topics that are meaningful to students is a powerful way to do this. They know these things, she said, based on their own educational experiences, the pedagogy classes they have taken, and their own teaching experiences. Many teachers are already using data in their classes, said Joshua Rosenberg (University of Tennessee, Knoxville). A survey found that 80 percent of K–12 science teachers already use student-collected data, and teachers also use primary source data and curated data. They work with data of varying sizes and use a variety of tools to support this work. Only a very small percentage of teachers (3.9%) report being not interested in professional development related to working with data. However, said Rosenberg, there are opportunities to do more. These opportunities include using tools other than spreadsheets, expanding beyond visualizing data and toward modeling data, and using data as a bridge between math and science classes. On the last point, Rosenberg said that while it takes time and effort to co-develop materials that are both mathematically and scientifically meaningful, data science is an effective way to serve the learning objectives of both math and science. Leticia Perez (WestEd) said that when it comes to data science, science teachers "don't need to buy in." Once teachers are introduced to tools and techniques they can use to bring data to life in the classroom, they are excited and willing. The key, said Perez, is to support natural entry points and areas in which data science connects to the existing goals and learning objectives of the class.

Vision for Teacher Preparation

Given the current state, H. Lee asked panelists to envision what teacher preparation *should* look like, and to identify the skills and practices teachers need to effectively teach data science. Anna Bargagliotti (Loyola Marymount University) began by noting that K–12 data science looks different than undergraduate or professional data science; the goal is to develop some level of data acumen in all students. Bargagliotti said that the framework of the *Pre-K–12 Guidelines for Assessment and Instruction in Statistics Education II* (GAISE II)[3] is relevant to this goal and highlighted a few specifics. First, GAISE II emphasizes the importance of working with multiple variables and multivariate thinking as early as kindergarten, she said. Second, the framework promotes the concept that data science is a process that can be guided by "questioning, questioning, questioning" throughout the data cycle. When focusing on teacher preparation, said Bargagliotti, it is important to build these skills and give teachers these experiences, with data that are relevant to them. She noted that just as data science education needs to be engaging and relevant for students, the same is true for teachers. There are opportunities in all disciplines to find rich and interesting data for teachers to manipulate, investigate, and interrogate.

Anne Leftwich (Indiana University Bloomington) said that in her experience working with teachers, many do not believe that data science, computer science, or technology apply to them or their classes. For example, a primary school teacher might say that data science is more appropriate for secondary school, while a social studies teacher might say that data science is more appropriate for a science or math class. Due to this challenge, Leftwich agreed with Bargagliotti that teacher preparation must be relevant to teachers' content area and grade level and must show examples that they can achieve. For example, teacher preparation for elementary teachers can emphasize how data science can help young students process the world around them and lead to a stronger understanding of math and problem-solving practices, whereas teacher preparation for physical education teachers can emphasize how data science can help students improve their understanding of their own health. This can be accomplished all in one class, said Leftwich, but it is critical to have accessible tools, appropriate datasets, and subject-specific examples that are relevant to each area.

Before teachers can teach data science, said Gemma Mojica (North Carolina State University), they need experience engaging with data. They need to engage in the entire process, from asking questions, to collecting or considering data, to exploring the data with tools, and to using the data to answer questions and communicate what they have found. Speakers at the

[3]https://www.amstat.org/asa/files/pdfs/GAISE/GAISEIIPreK-12_Full.pdf

workshop have discussed the need for students to be "awash in data," to explore complex and messy datasets, and to learn how to use data science tools, said Mojica. These are the same skills and experiences that teachers need to have themselves before they can envision how to create a learning environment that engages students in these practices.

Perez added that part of teacher preparation is creating awareness around where and how data science can be brought to the classroom. She noted that domains are often siloed in elementary school; for example, students are looking at bar graphs in math class and six months later are looking at the same types of data visualizations in a science unit on the weather. This is a missed opportunity, said Perez, and there is a need to help teachers become aware of the potential for alignment and synergy between domains.

Preservice Teacher Education

H. Lee asked panelists to comment on how the pipeline of new teachers can be prepared to teach data science by participating in preservice teacher education. Casey said that there are three key areas in which change is necessary to effectively train the next generation of teachers. First, teacher educators—including content course teachers, methods course teachers, and mentor teachers—need professional development. Second, preservice teachers need meaningful clinical experiences involving the teaching of data science. Casey noted that it is extremely challenging to find placements with a mentor teacher who can help develop the preservice teacher's skills, knowledge, and disposition in data science, let alone in a school that includes data science in the curriculum. Third, teacher preparation standards largely drive what happens in teacher preparation programs, and teachers take assessments at the end of their program to demonstrate their competency in teaching. If data science is not included in the standards or the assessments, it will remain challenging to incorporate it in preservice education. Bargagliotti agreed that accreditation and licensure standards are a barrier to training preservice teachers in data science education. She put out a "call to action" to workshop participants who are in math departments to do their best to build data science and statistics curriculum into preservice teaching curricula so that teachers begin to see the value in data science and demand professional development in this area. However, to make progress, said Bargagliotti, "we are at a point" where there is a need to push for accreditation standards to include statistics and data science.

In-service Teacher Education

H. Lee asked, once teachers are licensed and in the classroom, what are some creative ways that practicing teachers can gain skills and knowledge about data science education? Mojica observed that there are a number of different models that can be used to engage teachers in professional learning. There is evidence that supports very intense work at a local level with small groups of teachers. However, she said, some teachers may be the only teacher of data or statistics in the entire district, or may be a long distance from colleagues, so other models are needed. Massive open online courses (MOOCs) have been created for teacher educators, and there is evidence that these courses had a positive impact on teachers' confidence, beliefs, and practices. There is a need to consider these types of alternate models for professional development instead of pursuing a one-size-fits-all approach, said Mojica. There are opportunities for hybrid approaches that blend online learning experiences with face-to-face engagement, and for using other platforms and spaces to personalize learning for teachers in a way that is accessible and meets their needs. Perez said that in order to engage teachers in in-service preparation for data science education, there is a need to reach out and communicate with stakeholders such as administrators and district leadership. Intentional conversations with leaders at different levels, she said, will help them understand the connections between data science and educational standards. Further, conversations and professional development need to happen in a transdisciplinary space and need to include a broad group of stakeholders.

Research on Teacher Preparation

H. Lee asked panelists to describe the existing research on teacher preparation for data science education and to identify areas where there are research gaps. One thing we know about teacher learning, said Leftwich, is that teachers want to find ways to make an impact on their students and their learning. If teachers believe that data science is important and it will help their students engage in and learn the subject matter, teachers will want to incorporate it into their classroom. She emphasized that while conversations about preparation tend to focus on the knowledge that teachers need, it is just as important to improve their attitude and self-efficacy. Particularly at the elementary level, said Leftwich, teachers can be hesitant about their ability to teach technology or data science; it is critical to build confidence and provide them with tools and models that allow them to easily move ideas into practice.

Rosenberg said that there are research findings from other fields that can illuminate our understanding of how to best prepare teachers for data science education: for example, teachers do well when they have a chance to try activities with supportive peers, when they have sustained opportunities to receive feedback from peers or a coach, and when they can adapt curriculum materials. H. Lee shared other findings from research on teacher learning. First, teachers learn best when the subject is connected to their practice and their goals for their students. Second, teachers care about student learning, so it can be useful to have examples that show what is possible and how an activity might look in the classroom. Third, said H. Lee, research shows that teachers find frameworks "incredibly useful." Professional learning is most successful when teachers can situate their learning within a framework and can see how their professional learning goals and progress fit within the framework. H. Lee encouraged those who design teacher professional learning to make the underlying framework explicit to the teachers rather than keeping the design at the design table.

Challenges and Barriers

H. Lee asked, what are the challenges and systematic barriers that need to be addressed in order to make progress in teacher learning for data science? Casey focused on one specific aspect of the educational system that is creating barriers for data science: college admissions. She noted that colleges have long privileged calculus when making decisions about admissions and that students need calculus on their transcript to be competitive whether their program of study in college requires calculus. This is a big barrier, said Casey. In addition, colleges also look closely at how many AP classes a prospective student has taken, and there is currently no AP data science class. Although there is an Advanced Placement (AP) statistics class, it is "certainly not the type of data science we've been talking about at this workshop." Perez added that we need to expand the conversation and think about administrators and school site district leadership to help them understand connections to the standards.

Perez said that another challenge is a lack of stable descriptions of concepts such as data acumen, data habits of mind, and data fluency. There is a need for shared understanding so that teachers can communicate across disciplines and projects. Rosenberg agreed that clarity is needed on what data science is; for example, teachers may want to do more than data visualization but aren't sure what the next step is. Leftwich said that in order to move data science forward, there is a need for more readily accessible and free software that allows students and teachers to use and manipulate data easily. Particularly at the elementary level, there is a need for user-friendly tools that allow students to upload their own data and manipulate the data to tell a story.

Audience Q&A

Existing Courses

Strode asked panelists about the specific courses that are being offered to preservice teachers in universities around the country and in which departments they are situated. Mojica said that there is a class at North Carolina State University that is in both the College of Education and the Department of Statistics, and it focuses on the teaching and learning of statistics. Creating a class like this requires talking to colleagues in other departments and being creative, she said, but this type of collaboration is necessary for a transdisciplinary subject like data science. Bargagliotti said that she has heard from several educators who are teaching classes in colleges to future teachers based on her book *Statistics and Data Science for Teachers*; these classes are situated in statistics, education, and math departments. Casey said that she is aware of data science being integrated into a number of different courses, including classes on statistics, teaching with technology, social context of education, and education equity. In some of these classes, data science is a "grain-sized" module that is integrated, and in others, data are used as an integral part of learning throughout. For example, preservice teachers may use tools like CODAP to investigate real data (e.g., data on inequality in education). Research has shown that these experiences are meaningful and can improve teachers' confidence and knowledge, said Mojica. The particular classes and departments where data science is taught can vary widely depending on programs and interest of faculty members, said Leftwich. Ultimately, if teacher educators buy in to the importance of data science and understand what it can look like in the classroom, data science can be integrated in multiple ways and areas, she said.

Shifting Course Requirements

Given the discussion earlier in the session about how requirements for teacher education largely drive the curriculum, Melville asked panelists if and how these requirements might be changed to require courses in data science education. "Is that something worth making a noise about," she asked, or is it best to continue on the path to infusing it into existing courses? Melville noted that in her personal experience, required courses outside her subject matter felt contrived and like tasks that just needed to be checked off her list. What kind of work is being done to shift that perspective and to embrace and value transdisciplinary practices? H. Lee said that in North Carolina, the state requires secondary teachers to take a computing course. Historically, North Carolina State University required it to be a course in Java programming, but recently it has opened up to allow courses on R or Python. Sometimes there are broad recommendations at the state level, said H. Lee, that can be creatively interpreted by the university. Rosenberg added that he would like to learn from the computing education world how it has addressed the issue of state requirements to see if lessons could be applied to data science education. Perez noted that there is a critical teacher shortage right now, and while this is an unfortunate situation, it opens up potential opportunities. She explained that nontraditional routes toward licensure have more flexibility than traditional teacher preparation programs and requirements, and there may be opportunities to infuse data science in these spaces. Rosenberg agreed and added that attention should be paid to teachers who are being prepared outside of teacher education programs.

5

Looking Forward

In the final sessions of the workshop, participants reflected on the presentations and discussions, and identified areas in which more research or work is needed.

RESEARCH

On both days of the workshop, a "townhall" session was held to explore and discuss research needs for data science education. The first townhall was aimed at identifying the highest priorities for additional research, and the second townhall was designed to explore how practice can inform current and future research needs. Each session was moderated by a member of the planning committee, who invited in-person and virtual workshop participants to share their experiences, thoughts, and questions.

Townhall Day 1: What Are the Highest Priorities for Additional Research?

At the end of the first day, M. Wilkerson began the townhall session by asking workshop participants to reflect on the discussions throughout the day at the workshop, and to use these as a jumping-off point for identifying priorities for additional research in the area of data science education (see Box 5-1 for a summary of participant-identified priorities).

It is evident from the discussions at this workshop, said Santo, that there are a wide range of motivations, purposes, rationales, and potential outcomes for data science in K–12 education. Rather than treating these aspects like background information and immediately moving on to the

BOX 5-1
List of Participant-identified Priorities for Research, Development, and Resources

- Rationales for data science and how/whether these rationales fit with outcomes and design (Santo)
- Resources for data literacy, in particular connecting data with social justice (Bertram)
- Ensuring that students can present their work in a meaningful and impactful way (Holbert)
- Identifying and creating datasets that are appropriate for classroom use (Manchester)
- Learning lessons from similar work that has been done in the world of computer science (Weintrop)
- Getting buy-in from districts, states, and policymakers to make room for data science (McEnearney)
- Applications of critical data literacy in relation to student and teacher perceptions of mathematical identities and transference of mathematics to their communities (virtual participant)
- Viable ways to have common underlying habits of mind and processes that may just look different from one tool to another (in the use of tools that are currently geared toward teaching, learning, data literacy, and data science) (virtual participant)

design of programs, Santo encouraged stakeholders to make these an object of inquiry in order to clearly articulate them. For example, what are the different purposes of data literacy and data science, and how do these differences impact the way they are taught and the desired outcomes? It is important, he said, to be intentional and clear about the rationale behind teaching data science and not to take rationales at face value. For example, one rationale for teaching data literacy might be that it would eliminate issues such as vaccine resistance; however, the research on motivated reasoning suggests that this is unlikely to be the case. Making rationales an object of inquiry allows us to then consider how different rationales lead to different designs and institutional arrangements, said Santo; the rationale, purpose, and objectives should completely shape the design of the intervention.

Carol Bertram, a high school teacher in Chicago, offered her request that more work be done to connect math and statistics to social awareness and social justice. Bertram said that she gets "a lot of leeway" in the data science class she teaches, but she currently is on her own to find data, develop questions, and figure out how to engage students. She said she would love to see more prepared resources and curricula for teachers on data literacy, particularly given our experiences during the pandemic.

There has been a lot of discussion about ensuring that datasets and inquiries are relevant, authentic, and important to students, said Nathan Holbert (Teachers College, Columbia University). Several speakers have emphasized the importance of engaging students in inquiries that matter to them, their communities, and the world, he said. The missing piece, however, is enabling students to share their discoveries in a legitimate and impactful way. Holbert noted that when students have the opportunity to present their projects, it is often in a perfunctory manner. There is a need, he said, to make sure that the voices of these passionate learners can be heard in a way that gives them agency to change their world using data.

Data science education requires datasets, said Manchester. Although the Library of Congress has digital collections available, the datasets tend to be raw, very big, or in complex formats that require modification. There are different needs for datasets, depending on whether they are for pedagogical purposes or research purposes. It takes a lot of work to create data that are appropriate for classroom use, and we are still figuring out exactly how to do this, she said. More research in this area is needed.

Coming into this workshop from a background in computer science, said David Weintrop (University of Maryland), it is clear that there are a lot of overlapping challenges, issues, and opportunities between data science and computer science. Some of the questions being asked—about the goals of data science education, the role of tools, the role of industry, and the potential for integration with other disciplines—are questions that were explored for computer science education 10 or 15 years ago. Although data science is distinct from computer science in some ways, said Weintrop, there are also many similarities that offer the opportunity to learn from the experiences in that field. "It would be a real shame" if the field of data science was still struggling to answer some of these questions a decade from now, he said. Weintrop encouraged stakeholders to think critically about where data science education overlaps with other disciplines and where it is unique in order to identify where lessons could be learned. For example, integrating computer science into preservice teacher methods classes has been a struggle; the field of data science can learn from these experiences and lessons.

The work that needs to be done, said Colleen McEnearney (Tuva), is not in convincing teachers to buy in to data science education but in persuading districts and policymakers of its importance. McEnearney said she would have loved to use data science tools and techniques in her years as a high school math teacher, but she felt constrained by all of the requirements and testing that had to happen. In her experience, teachers would be excited to learn how to integrate data science into their classes, but they feel that "their hands are tied" by the state. There is a need to work with districts and policymakers to make room for data science in K–12 education, she said. Alternatively, it may be time to be "more radical" and advocate as a community for a different system for our students.

Townhall Day 2: How Can Practice Inform Current and Future Research Needs?

At the end of the second day, Horton asked workshop participants to think holistically, broadly, and in a "visionary fashion" about how teaching practice can inform current and future research needs in the area of data science education based on the discussions throughout the day, and then opened the floor for conversation (see Box 5-2 for a summary of participant-identified needs that are informed by teaching practice).

Steve Leinwand (American Institute for Research) began the session by asking to broaden the perspective beyond practice to include experiences, products, and perspectives. Leinwand described himself as a former "hippie math teacher" and a "self-proclaimed mathematics education change agent." Based on his experiences through the years, Leinwand emphasized

BOX 5-2
List of Participant-identified Needs Informed by Teaching Practice Discussions

- Clear conceptualization of data science education that is created by a diverse group of stakeholders (Leinwand)
- Changes on multiple levels, from state to district, not just teacher training (Teasley)
- Research on progression of data skills in K–12, appropriate assessments, and how and where to focus supportive professional learning (virtual participant)
- Assessment of what students are learning when they learn data science (Gould)
- Research exploring the tension between integrating data science and teaching it as a standalone subject (Schweingruber)
- Understanding of the experiences and capacities of teachers (V. Lee)
- An assets approach in which students' natural interest in sorting and classifying their world is leveraged for data science education (in-person participant)
- Consideration of how data science education would translate into rural school districts that have limited access to technology, the Internet, and specialized teachers (in-person participant)
- Consideration of how to approach data science education in subpopulations such as special education and those who are neurodivergent (Perez)
- Research on the knowledge, skills, and dispositions that teachers need in order to teach data science effectively (virtual participant)

the importance of clarifying exactly what is meant by K–12 data science. He analogized it to the Bay Area Writing Project,[1] in which writing is taught from kindergarten through 12th grade and infused throughout. Data science needs to be conceptualized the same way. Data science needs a two-page explanation, he said, as well as a 50-plus-page document making the case for data science and data literacy. These documents need to be created by a broad, diverse group of stakeholders, including researchers, teachers, future educators, data scientists, and mathematicians, he said.

Gould agreed with the need for further clarification about the goals of conceptual understanding and statistics, and the need for a better understanding of issues such as the role of provenance, the synthesis of the investigative process with technology, and the ethical and societal implications. There is a need for a curriculum-agnostic and tool-agnostic assessment of what students are learning when they are learning data science. With this knowledge, he said, we could make a better argument to universities about the value of data science education and how it prepares students for higher education and the workforce. Louie suggested that one way to begin to understand these issues would be to survey existing data science courses to see what learning objectives have been identified. Heidi Schweingruber (the National Academies of Sciences, Engineering, and Medicine) said that along with research on the learning objectives of data science, research is needed to explore the tension between data science as a standalone subject and data science as a topic integrated into other disciplines. Some speakers have advocated for adding data science as a subject into schools, whereas others have advocated for using data science to solve problems and improve learning in existing disciplines. There are learning and teaching questions related to this tension, she said, such as the following: Do the skills and knowledge of data science exist outside of the content being interrogated? If so, to what extent are they abstract, and how can assessments best capture these skills and knowledge?

The impediments to data science education are far larger than what can be addressed in teacher training, said Stephanie Teasley (University of Michigan School of Information). Changes need to be made at multiple levels, including changes to state standards for licensure, district-level changes to curriculum, shifts in how high school counselors and college admissions officers think about data science, and increases in the accessibility of data tools. Until and unless these changes are made, we will be "pushing the rock uphill," continued Teasley, even if teachers are motivated and prepared to teach data science.

On the topic of teachers, V. Lee said that an important research issue is the current circumstances and lived experiences of teachers with respect to teaching data science. In the two days that participants have been at this

[1]https://bawp.berkeley.edu/

workshop, he said, typical teachers "have seen 160 students and put out 250 fires." They are being asked to do socioemotional learning in the midst of a pandemic and recovery and, in some places, to do hybrid instruction without extra pay or support. Now we are asking them to integrate data, computing, and technology into the classroom, said V. Lee; how much are we asking, and can we support teachers in these efforts? Horton agreed that this is an important point and said that we need to consider what will be sustainable, what supports are needed, and where the point of exhaustion is.

FUNDING

"This is just the beginning of our work together," said Nancy Lue (Valhalla Foundation). From the perspective of a philanthropist, Lue said that she sees a number of opportunities to chart a path forward for data science education. She shared three key takeaways from the workshop that are relevant to the issue of funding. First, the field needs more evidence on what is working and how to scale it. Lue noted that while the K–12 data science movement is quite nascent, there is a lot of momentum and many promising innovations; there is a need to accelerate research to better understand what is working, develop a clear evidence base of the impact, and scale the promising practices and programs to ensure that all students are able to succeed in a data-rich world. In particular, she said, there is a need to advance research on assessments, on student-level outcomes, and on the best ways to prepare and support educators. Second, the "promise and perils" of data mean that we must start developing data literacy skills for all students, starting with the earliest learners, using a student-centered approach that spans all of K–12. This may include standalone data science courses, data science that is integrated into other courses, or both. In addition, there is a need for a clear bridge to postsecondary education. Third, said Lue, as the field evolves, the needs of the most marginalized students need to be kept at the forefront, and programs, resources, and tools need to meet the needs of our diverse student population in an inclusive and equitable manner. Lue said that this is an "exciting juncture" for the field of data science education and invited two other funders to make remarks.

Ulrich Boser (Schmidt Futures) said that Schmidt Futures, which focuses on raising and supporting talent to solve pressing problems, has made several investments to improve the pipeline for data science. One of the interesting things about the data science field, he said, is that people can be considered experts at a young age, purely because of their expertise and abilities. This is clearly very different from other fields where a Ph.D. is the bare minimum to be considered an expert. Boser identified two key challenges that need to be addressed in data science in order to make progress.

First, he said, how can these "incredibly exciting" demonstration projects be scaled across the nation? Second, there is a need to bring together people from diverse backgrounds—including those from both sides of the political aisle—in order to come to a shared understanding of data science and grapple with how to implement it in K–12 education.

The California Education Learning Lab, said Lark Park (California Education Learning Lab), is a state-funded higher education grant program that funds faculty doing innovative work to improve learning outcomes and close equity gaps at the three large public systems. Most of the funding has been dedicated to improving STEM education at the postsecondary level, which included some data science projects. There is a lot of overlap between the discussions at this workshop and the discussions happening at the Learning Lab, she said, and there is a close relationship between K–12 education and higher education. For example, as other speakers have noted, higher education sets expectations and opportunities for students pursuing postsecondary pathways by setting admissions standards and giving credit for courses. Park said that she looks forward to deepening this relationship and working together. One of the most exciting things about the workshop, she said, has been the emphasis on student agency and student voice, and the acknowledgment that data science presents an opportunity for students to understand, critique, and engage in the world. Park shared a recent grant opportunity from the Learning Lab that focuses on data science. After offering general grants for STEM, as well as specific grants for calculus reform, the Learning Lab became interested in creating an opportunity for data science because of its importance to other disciplines, the workforce, and productive citizens of the world. The Learning Lab announced a Grand Challenge in Building Critical Mass for Data Science[2] to help create an inflection point in data science education. There are multiple opportunities available, including opportunities for faculty development, pathway development, and interdisciplinary collaboration. While this grant is targeted at California institutions, California is a big state and "what we do here can matter." Park said that university and community college faculty are the target audience, but it is strongly encouraging collaboration with high schools.

REFLECTIONS

In the closing session of the workshop, planning committee members offered their reflections on the discussions held at the workshop, identified key takeaway messages, and identified possible next steps for the field. H. Lee began the reflection session with an observation that the idea of co-design was frequently mentioned during the workshop, and she encouraged

[2]https://calearninglab.org/grant/data-science-rfp/

stakeholders to consider ways to bring teacher voices and student voices into their work. When planning teacher professional learning, teachers can be brought in as co-designers and become part of the team. When designing a tool for educational use, the student and teacher experience with using the tool should be kept front-and-center.

Clegg asked, "What is the end goal of data science education?" There are several overlapping and discrete goals, including training students to be data scientists and helping students become data-literate members of society. The broadness of data science requires developing a broad view of what counts as expertise and pulling from a diverse pool of expertise to support learners and teachers. For example, said Clegg, teachers from different disciplines, librarians, community members, and artists all have expertise that can be used to create learning opportunities for students. This diverse pool can also serve as resources, support, and collaborators for educators. Clegg said there is a need to think about new models of student learning and professional development that are able to leverage this expertise, both in and out of the school context.

Erickson gave workshop participants a brief "optimistic historical perspective." He said that the field of data science has been around for only about 10 years. To people of a certain age, 10 years "is nothing." But looking around the room, he noted that there were many young people to whom "10 years is a lifetime." This is "fantastic" because it means that young researchers and young educators are getting involved in the field; he said he was "so glad" to see them there.

As one of the youngest people in the room, Drozda said that it has been an incredible honor to be involved in these conversations. He offered three observations about K–12 students and presented a brief framework of three practices to consider. First, he said, students today are inundated with data, from TikTok to Twitter. It is not a winning proposition to take away their phones or laptops because "you can't win." These are not distractions; instead, they are the tools of the future. Second, Drozda said that the cost to acquire information is "close to zero today," which means that simply memorizing facts or formulas is not very valuable for students. Third, with the immense quality of online content consumed by children today, the bar for what is relevant or authentic has risen quite high. Drozda said that students have an "increasingly precise radar" for what is relevant versus what is corny, fake, or overly modified for the classroom. Throughout the workshop, he said, we have seen examples of how relevant, authentic data can engage students. Drozda offered three practices to keep in mind as new programs are considered. First, prove relevance to students up front, and tell them explicitly why the content matters. Second, pick topics that are not just relevant but also recent; "we need to be thinking of last week or last night." Third, pacing is critical. Drozda said, "We have to create an aura of speed while trying to engage in content depth."

What has been striking about this workshop, said Matuk, is how many learners and teachers across various subjects and contexts are already engaging in data literacy and data science, whether or not they are aware of it. In addition, data science is already naturally integrated in the professional work of many fields, including biology, social science, and journalism. Instead of trying to find places for data science in classes, Matuk suggested that stakeholders consider how to make learning experiences "more authentic to those domains in and of themselves." That is, instead of teaching data science for its own sake, she said that educators should integrate data science because it is an integral part of the domain that is being taught.

Horton shared his reflections on the two days of the workshop. First, he noted that there is "tremendous excitement and enthusiasm" in the area of data science; although there are huge challenges ahead, we have the energy to tackle them, and this is the time to make a difference. Horton emphasized that one area that needs to be thought about is the levels at which students should be prepared to do certain things. From an academic statistics standpoint, the Ph.D. is the "pinnacle of some kind of pyramid," and there has been work on building master's programs as well. However, Horton said there is a need to think about how to prepare students with bachelor's or associate's degrees as well; he stated, "We can't afford people to go through four years of expensive higher education and not do useful things." Another opportunity, he said, is to do work on defining data science and associated terms like data literacy, data fluency, and data acumen. Using existing learning outcomes to begin to shape these definitions would be a good start, he said. Teacher preparation is a major challenge that will require major changes such as breaking down siloes, building new partnerships and bridges, and aligning incentives. In all the work that lies ahead, Horton emphasized that accessibility, diversity, equity, and inclusion must be at the forefront. In particular, the data divide must be addressed; it is critical to the future of the country and the work we are doing. On this point, he shared two quotes from the National Science Foundation report *Keeping Data Science Broad:*[3]

> *Consequently, as data-driven decision-making becomes more commonplace, having the skills to understand and make sense of data can provide a sense of power to the larger citizenry or conversely powerlessness to communities without these skills. This "Data Divide" separates communities that have access to devices and services that provide rich, data-driven*

[3]https://par.nsf.gov/biblio/10075971-keeping-data-science-broadnegotiating-digital-data-divide-among-higher-educationinstitutions

> *services from those that don't; it separates data-savvy individuals, and communities that have understanding and awareness of how their data is being collected and used to provide individualized services (and thus informed protections), from those that do not. The economic and social consequences of the Data Divide stratify populations, and severely limit the opportunities of those who are unable to take advantage of the data revolution. (Page 7)*
>
> *If we do not make diversity and inclusion a priority now, we will not have it in the future. We do not want to repeat the mistakes of the past, so we must reverse the trend for the growing divide to make and keep data science broad. Diversity will bring a lot of ideas and voices to the table, which may lead to significantly fewer models producing biased results when trained using algorithms on biased data sets. (Page 30)*

M. Wilkerson closed out the workshop with her reflections. First, she emphasized that there are multiple types of data expertise and multiple types of data experts. Whereas there is a pattern of talking about those experts with a Ph.D. in statistics, or those who end up at Google, other professionals—including journalists, biologists, and geoscientists—are deeply engaged with data. She encouraged stakeholders to think about these different areas of expertise and how these pathways can be made visible and accessible to students. "When we broaden what it means to be successful in data science," she said, it invites students in and broadens their possible futures. M. Wilkerson's second point was to rethink what is meant by success and failure. Although we want to avoid the false promises of the power of data, she said, we want to present a nuanced view of how data fit into the advocacy toolkit, along with tools such as storytelling and organizing. Finally, collaboration is critical for the changes that are needed in this area. This includes collaboration among teachers; across levels of education administration; and with community members, librarians, practicing scientists, and others. Building and sustaining these collaborations will require incentives and supports, she said, such as time, encouragement, and opportunity for teachers to pursue the skills and knowledge that it takes to teach data science to their students.

References

Amrhein, V., Trafimow, D., and Greenland, S. (2019). Inferential statistics as descriptive statistics: There is no replication crisis if we don't expect replication. *The American Statistician, 73*(Suppl1), 262–270. https://doi.org/10.1080/00031305.2018.1543137

Lee, C., and Soep, E. (2023). *Code for What?* MIT Press. https://mitpress.mit.edu/9780262047456/code-for-what/

National Academies of Sciences, Engineering, and Medicine. (2021). *Cultivating Interest and Competencies in Computing: Authentic Experiences and Design Factors.* The National Academies Press. https://doi.org/10.17226/25912

———. (2018). *Data Science for Undergraduates: Opportunities and Options.* The National Academies Press. https://doi.org/10.17226/25104

National Academy of Engineering and National Research Council. (2014). *STEM Integration in K–12 Education: Status, Prospects, and an Agenda for Research.* The National Academies Press. https://doi.org/10.17226/18612

National Research Council. (2012). *A Framework for K–12 Science Education: Practices, Crosscutting Concepts, and Core Ideas.* The National Academies Press. https://doi.org/10.17226/13165

Podworny, S., Fleischer, Y., Hüsing, S., Biehler, R., Frischemeier, D., Höper, L., and Schulte, C. (2021). Using data cards for teaching data based decision trees in middle school. *21st Koli Calling International Conference on Computing Education Research* (Koli Calling '21), November 18–21, 2021, Joensuu, Finland. Association for Computing Machinery. https://doi.org/10.1145/3488042.3489966

Appendix A

Workshop Agenda

Foundations of Data Science for Students in Grades K–12: A Workshop

All Times are EST.

Purpose:

To bring increasing visibility to the rapidly growing field of K–12 data science education, this workshop will survey the current landscape of work, surface what is currently known, and identify additional research to support student learning, curriculum and tools development, assessment, and the preparation of educators. The workshop will bring together researchers and practitioners engaged in K–12 data science education from a variety of contexts including formal and informal; designed and emergent; elementary and secondary; and whose efforts include standalone curricula as well as activities integrated within other content areas (e.g., STEM disciplines and the humanities).

DAY 1: TUESDAY, SEPTEMBER 13, 2022

10:00–10:05 AM **Welcome from the National Academies**
Heidi Schweingruber, *Director, Board on Science Education*

10:05–10:20 AM	**Opening Remarks and Workshop Framing** Nicholas Horton (co-chair), *Amherst College* Michelle Hoda Wilkerson (co-chair), *University of California, Berkeley*
10:20–11:20 AM	**A Vision for High-Quality Data Science Education** This session will explore what defines a valuable learning experience for students, what research tells us about successful vs. unsuccessful curricular intervention, and how those learnings can be articulated into policy and practice. **Moderator:** Michelle Hoda Wilkerson, *University of California, Berkeley* **Panelists:** • Rob Gould, *University of California, Los Angeles* • Josh Recio, *Dana Center* • Tricia Shelton, *National Science Teaching Association* • Alfred Spector, *Massachusetts Institute of Technology* (virtual) • Trena Wilkerson, *Baylor University; National Council of Teachers of Mathematics*
11:20–11:45 AM	**Networking Break**
11:45 AM–12:45 PM	**Where and How Is Data Science Happening?** The goal of this session is to explore the research on the settings and contexts of K–12 data science education with an emphasis on what data science looks like in these contexts and the connections with informal contexts relevant to K–12 learners' lives. **Moderator:** Tammy Clegg, *University of Maryland* **Panelists:** • Marshini Chetty, *University of Chicago* (virtual) • Kayla DesPortes, *New York University* • Rafi Santo, *Telos Learning* • Stephen Uzzo, *New York Hall of Science*
12:45–1:45 PM	**Working Lunch: What Are the Outcomes That We Want?** Lunch will be provided. During lunch, participants will be broken up into small groups to discuss

the outcomes that we want for data science education. These could be student-level outcomes (e.g., developing specific skills and proficiencies, developing interest or disciplinary identity) or outcomes related to policy and practice (e.g., access to opportunities, funding). As part of the discussion, also consider the research that is needed to further what is known about these outcomes.

Virtual Audience: We are not facilitating breakout groups. We invite you to share your ideas in this document: Virtual Outcomes. You are welcome to provide your name next to your suggestion, but it is not required. Ideas provided in this document will be incorporated into the next session and will also be available on the project page following the event.

1:45–2:45 PM **Invited Commentary on Outcomes and Report Out from Working Groups**

This session will explore the evidence on what we know about learning and critical data literacy (and outcomes identified by participants) to consider what it is that we want students to be able to do with data and identify how those intended outcomes can be measured.

Background Readings:

A Secret Agent. K–12 Data Science Learning Through the Lens of Agency[1]

Critical Data Literacy: Creating a More Just World with Data[2]

Moderator: Nicholas Horton, *Amherst College*

Presenters:

- Ryan "Seth" Jones, *Middle Tennessee State University*
- Jo Louie, *Education Development Center, Inc.*

Discussant: Jo Boaler, *Stanford University* (virtual)

2:45–3:00 PM **Break**

---

[1]Available at https://www.nationalacademies.org/event/09-13-2022/docs/DD667E469D0EC5DD91A7D85BC839A9852491A3CF9F15

[2]Available at https://www.nationalacademies.org/event/09-13-2022/docs/D16254F310D01BBDA873920E4EFB8151F2D8334181AA

3:00–4:00 PM **How Are Tools and Resources Supporting Data Science Learning Experiences?**
Through this session, there will be an exploration of the tools and data sets that exist or are needed to support learning in acquiring data understanding and skills.
Background Reading: Tools to Support Data Analysis and Data Science in K–12 Education[3]
Moderator: Tim Erickson, *Epistemological Engineering*
Panelists:

- Rolf Biehler, *Paderborn University, Germany* (virtual)
- Chad Dorsey, *Concord Consortium*
- Randy Kochevar, *Education Development Center, Inc.*
- Victor Lee, *Stanford Graduate School of Education*
- Andee Rubin, *TERC*

4:00–4:25 PM **Townhall**

4:25–4:30 PM **Adjournment and Plan for Day 2**
Michelle Hoda Wilkerson (co-chair), *University of California, Berkeley*
Nicholas Horton (co-chair), *Amherst College*

END OF DAY 1

DAY 2: WEDNESDAY, SEPTEMBER 14, 2022

10:00–10:15 AM **Welcome and Reflections on Day 1**
Michelle Hoda Wilkerson (co-Chair), *University of California, Berkeley*
Nicholas Horton (co-Chair), *Amherst College*

---

[3]Available at https://www.nationalacademies.org/event/09-13-2022/docs/DB48F8A34F71C395C3071BABFFD42AFFF06478824419

10:15–11:15 AM **Hearing from Practice: What Is Happening in and out of Schools?**
This session will explore the reality on the ground in data science education, with a deep focus on the specifics of designing student learning opportunities. Topics will include student learning progressions, opportunities for different school subjects to impart data science topics, and the wraparound resources needed for implementation.
Background Reading: Previewing the National Landscape of K–12 Data Science Implementation[4]
Moderator: Zarek Drozda, *Director, Data Science 4 Everyone, University of Chicago*
Panelists:
- Suyen Machado, *University of California, Los Angeles*
- Stephanie Melville, *San Diego Unified School District*
- Paul Strode, *Fairview High School*
- Katie Headrick Taylor, *University of Washington*

11:15–11:30 AM **Break**

11:30 AM – 12:30 PM **How Is Data Science Integrated in Content Areas?**
This session will explore the ways in which data science has been integrated with other subjects beyond mathematics. Panelists will share, through discussions of their own and related work, approaches for integrating data science into the study of other subjects as they are explored across settings including school-based and out-of-school contexts.
Moderator: Camillia Matuk, *New York University* (virtual)
Panelists:
- Rahul Bhargava, *Northeastern University*
- Angela Calabrese Barton, *University of Michigan*

[4]Available at https://www.nationalacademies.org/event/09-13-2022/docs/D688ED916E82498DA0E2171A109936D679FD5DE26556

- Josh Radinsky, *University of Illinois at Chicago*
- Emmanuel Schanzer, *Bootstrap*
- Lissa Soep, *Vox Media, LLC* (virtual)

12:30–1:30 PM **Lunch**

1:30–2:30 PM **What Is the State of Teacher Preparation in Data Science?**

The goal of this session is to examine issues on teachers' use of data and the preparation needed to teach statistics/data science/computation for prospective teachers and practicing teachers in formal and informal education settings.

Moderator: Hollylynne Lee, *North Carolina State University*

Panelists:

- Anna Bargagliotti, *Loyola Marymount University*
- Stephanie Casey, *Eastern Michigan University*
- Anne Leftwich, *Indiana University Bloomington* (virtual)
- Gemma Mojica, *North Carolina State University*
- Leticia Perez, *WestEd*
- Joshua Rosenberg, *University of Tennessee, Knoxville*

2:30–3:00 PM **Townhall**

3:00–3:15 PM **Funder Reflection**

Nancy Lue, *Valhalla Foundation*

Joined by:

- Ulrich Boser, *Schmidt Futures*
- Lark Park, *California Education Learning Lab* (virtual)

3:15–3:30 PM **Final Reflections from Planning Committee**

Nicholas Horton (co-chair), *Amherst College*

Michelle Hoda Wilkerson (co-chair), *University of California, Berkeley*

3:30 PM **WORKSHOP ADJOURNS**

Appendix B

Biographies of Committee Members and Presenters

Anna Bargagliotti (*Presenter,* she/her/hers) is a professor of mathematics in the Seaver College of Science and Engineering at Loyola Marymount University. She was the chair of the American Statistical Association/National Council of Teachers of Mathematics (ASA/NCTM) joint committee, a lead author on the jointly published ASA/NCTM GAISE II report, and an author on the ASA Statistical Education of Teachers report. She also co-authored the book *Statistics and Data Science for Teachers* with Christine Franklin. Bargagliotti's interests are in nonparametric and circular statistics, statistics education throughout the K–16 grade bands, data visualization, and multivariate models. She has received generous funding to carry out her research and has published dozens of research articles, columns, reports, OpEds, and book chapters. She is also the recipient of the ASA's Waller award, the Mu Sigma Rho's Warde award, the Dex Whittinghill award, and the Elizabeth and Michael Rudinica Prize. She received her Ph.D. at the University of California, Irvine in mathematics and her M.S. at the University of California, Los Angeles in statistics.

Rahul Bhargava (*Presenter*, he/him/his) is an educator, researcher, designer, and facilitator who builds collaborative projects to interrogate modern society with a focus on rethinking participation and power in data processes. He has created big data research tools to investigate media attention, built hands-on interactive museum exhibits, and ran over 100 workshops to build data culture in newsrooms, non-profits, and libraries. With Catherine D'Ignazio, he built Databasic.io, a suite of tools and activities that introduce learners to working with data. Bhargava has collaborated with a wide range of groups, from the state of Minas Gerais in Brazil, to the St. Paul library system, and even the World Food Program. His academic work on data literacy, technology, and civic media has been published in journals such as the *International Journal of Communication,* and *the Journal of Community Informatics*, and been presented at conferences such as IEEE VIS and the Association for the Advancement of Artificial Intelligence's International Conference on Weblogs and Social Media. His museum installations have appeared at the Boston Museum of Science, Eyebeam in New York City, and the Tech Interactive in San Jose. Bhargava is an assistant professor in journalism as well as art and design at Northeastern University, where he also directs the Data Culture Group.

Rolf Biehler (*Presenter*, he/him/his) is currently professor emeritus for didactics of mathematics at Paderborn University, Germany. He is currently a member of the International Collaboration for Research on Statistical Reasoning, Thinking and Literacy as well as the International Network for Didactic Research in University Mathematics scientific committee. Biehler is an editor or editorial board member in several book series and international journals for mathematics education. He has been co-directing the Project Data Science and Big Data at School (www.prodabi.de/en) since 2018, a collaborative project between computer science and statistics educators, which develops material for data science education including machine learning for primary, middle, and high school. Biehler and his team created the German localization of Fathom, TinkerPlots, and CODAP, and developed related classroom materials as well as empirical classroom studies. His research interests include probability, statistics, and data science education; university mathematics education; and the professional development of mathematics teachers. He has co-edited the 2022 Special Issue on data science education of the *Statistics Education Research Journal* and previously worked as a professor for didactics of mathematics at Kassel University before he moved to Paderborn University. He was a co-founder and co-director of the Centre for Research in University Mathematics Education (www.khdm.de/en). Biehler is engaged in the International Association of Statistics Education. He received his Ph.D. and habilitation in mathematics education from Bielefeld University.

Jo Boaler (*Presenter*, she/her/hers) is the Nomellini & Olivier Professor of Education at Stanford University. Her former roles have included being the Marie Curie Professor of Mathematics Education in England and a mathematics teacher in London comprehensive schools. Boaler has authored numerous books and articles and has been a White House presenter on women and girls. Her latest book is called *Limitless Mind: Learn, Lead and*

Live without Barriers. Boaler co-founded www.youcubed.org to give teachers, parents, and students the resources they need to excite students about mathematics. She is part of the writing team for the proposed Mathematics Framework for the state of California, is co-leading a K–12 Data Science Initiative, and was named as one of the eight educators "changing the face of education" by the BBC.

Angela Calabrese Barton (*Presenter*, she/her/hers) is a professor and chair of educational studies at the University of Michigan. She is currently a fellow of the American Educational Research Association (AERA) and is senior editor of the *American Educational Research Journal.* Her research focuses on designing and enacting equitable and socially just teaching of science in both schools and community organizations serving youth historically minoritized by dominant society. Calabrese Barton studies how these practices and approaches support youth in leveraging the content and practices of science as a context and tool for social transformation, with a particular focus on youth agency and identities. Her research takes a critical, participatory approach, involving youth, teachers, and community partners as co-researchers and co-designers, where they collaboratively seek to disrupt and transform systemic oppressions in science, schooling, and society. Calabrese Barton's research has been recognized by AERA with the 2018 Award for Exemplary Contributions to Practice-Engaged Research (AERA-wide), 2022 Award for Innovations in Research on Equity and Social Justice in Teacher Education (Division K), 2009 Award for Research Leading to Transformations of Social Contexts (Division G), and 2004 Exemplary Research Award in Teaching and Teacher Education (Division K). She is a former chemistry teacher and informal science educator; she continues to teach afterschool STEM in community makerspaces collaboratively with youth and university students as a part of her research and practice. Calabrese Barton has authored numerous books and articles, served as a WT Grant Distinguished Fellow, and was co-editor of the *Journal of Research in Science Teaching.*

Stephanie Casey (*Presenter*, she/her/hers) is a professor of mathematics education at Eastern Michigan University. She is currently a co-principal investigator on two National Science Foundation grants, ESTEEM and MODULE(S2), that have created statistics teacher education curriculum materials and accompanying professional development for mathematics teacher educators. Her research focuses on preparation for teaching statistics at the secondary level, motivated by her experience of teaching secondary mathematics.

Marshini Chetty (*Presenter*, she/her/hers) is an assistant professor in the Department of Computer Science at the University of Chicago where she directs the Amyoli Internet Research Laboratory (AIR lab). She specializes in human-computer interaction, usable privacy and security, and ubiquitous computing. Her work has won best paper awards at the Symposium on Usable Privery and Security Conference, Conference on Human Factors in Computing Systems, and Conference on Computer-Supported Cooperative Work and Social Computing, and she was a co-recipient of the Annual Privacy Papers for Policymakers award. Her research has been featured in the *New York Times*, CNN, *Washington Journal*, BBC, *Chicago Tribune*, *The Guardian*, *WIRED*, and Slashdot. She has received generous funding from the National Science Foundation, through grants and an National Science Foundation CAREER award, as well as the National Security Agency, Facebook, and multiple Google Faculty Research Awards.

Tamara L. Clegg (*Planning Committee Member*, she/her/hers) is an associate professor in the College of Information Studies at the University of Maryland, where she directs the new bachelor of arts degree in information design and co-directs the Youth eXperience Lab. Clegg's work focuses on designing technology (e.g., social media, mobile apps, e-textiles, community displays) to support life-relevant learning where learners, particularly those from underrepresented groups in science, engage in science in the context of achieving personally relevant goals. She seeks to understand ways such learning environments and technologies support scientific disposition development. Clegg's most recent work begins to explore critical data literacies among young learners and collegiate athletes in the context of everyday technology use and sports, respectively. Her work has been funded by the National Science Foundation, the Institute of Museum and Library Studies, and Google. She received her Ph.D. from Georgia Tech's College of Computing and her B.S. in computer science from North Carolina State University.

Kayla DesPortes (*Presenter*, she/her/hers) is an assistant professor of human-computer interaction and learning sciences at the New York University Steinhardt School of Culture, Education, and Human Development. She is a collaborative, community-centered researcher, designer, and engineer. DesPortes's work explores how artistic computing, engineering, and data literacy education can foster learners to leverage their knowledge and build new skills in order to empower themselves and their communities. She engages in long-term relationships with community partners and applies participatory methods that engage partners in agenda-setting, problem-solving, and integration of their knowledge and values into learning design. Furthermore, DesPortes centers equity in her investigations of the learning environment by examining how design with artistic practices can foster learners' and educators' engagement with cultures, identities, and the social and political dimensions of society.

Chad Dorsey (*Presenter*, he/him/his) is the president and CEO of the Concord Consortium, a non-profit organization dedicated to transforming STEM education through technology. His professional experience spans the fields of science, education, and technology, and he leads multiple projects researching the use of technology to support data science education and K–12 STEM learning. Dorsey currently heads several National Science Foundation–funded projects devoted to investigating cutting-edge topics in data science education research. He has been a consistent advocate for expanding research, pedagogy, and awareness of K–12 data science education. Across the past decade, Dorsey has helped catalyze the field of data science education by organizing coalitions, sponsoring convenings, and fostering field-building work. He is the founder of the Messy Data Coalition and a core steering member of the Data Science 4 Everyone coalition, and he currently leads an effort to develop a national portal of open datasets tailored for use in K–12 education and heads a nationwide project seeding a community of practice for data science education research.

Zarek D. Drozda (*Planning Committee Member*, he/him/his) is the director of Data Science 4 Everyone (DS4E), a national initiative and coalition based at the University of Chicago. He helped launch DS4E in 2019, co-organizing a coalition of now 1000+ education stakeholders across U.S. education. Drozda has continuously worked at the intersection of applied research, data, and policy. He served as a data science fellow for the U.S. Department of Education's Institute of Education Sciences, where he led research on data science, artificial intelligence, blockchain, and other emerging technology education for the agency. While working at the federal level, Drozda also advised the national COVID-19 response, running data analytics for an inter-agency team between the White House, Department of Education, and Centers for Disease Control and Prevention. He earned a bachelor's degree in economics from the University of Chicago, and he is very passionate about using data to tackle complex social problems.

Timothy E. Erickson (*Planning Committee Member*, he/him/his) develops curriculum and provides professional development for mathematics, science, and data education at the school level. He has primarily done this work as a freelancer, with occasional stints as a faculty member at the high school or college level. For the past few decades, most of this work has involved data education of some kind, ranging from modeling activities in physics to designing materials for introducing data science to high school students (https://concord.org/awashindata). Nearly all of Erickson's work recognizes the need for technology in data education, and has included creating software to help students collect and analyze data in various ways. Contracts with nonprofits such as The Concord Consortium have been his main source of funding; however, he has also received independent funding, including four Small Business Innovation Research awards from the National Science Foundation. Although he initially trained in astronomy and astrophysics at the California Institute of Technology and the University of California, Berkeley, Erickson was always interested in education, leading him to dedicate a large portion of his career to this pursuit.

Rob Gould (*Presenter*, he/him/his) is the vice-chair of undergraduate studies at the Deptartment of Statistics at the University of California, Los Angeles. He is the faculty advisor of the Introduction to Data Science project, a high school data science course. Gould is also founder of DataFest, an undergraduate data analysis competition and celebration of all things data that is held annually at over 40 universities and colleges around the world. With Rebecca Wong and Colleen Ryan, he is co-author of an introductory statistics book, *Exploring the World Through Data*, and was a co-author of the 2020 American Statistical Association and National Council of Teachers of Mathematics *Guidelines for Assessment and Instruction in Statistics Education*, pre-K–12 Report. Gould's research has been in the field of statistics education. He received his Ph.D. in mathematics from the University of California, San Diego.

Katie Headrick Taylor (*Presenter*, she/her/hers) is associate professor of learning sciences and human development at University of Washington's College of Education. Research-practice partnerships led by Taylor center racial and gender equity in STEM, data science, and digital literacy. These collaborations have occurred across museums, public libraries, public schools, homes, undergraduate courses, and family-serving organizations in New York, Chicago, Nashville, Seattle, and nonmetropolitan areas of East Tennessee. Her scholarship and teaching focus on community well-being through the digital re-mediation of learning, foregrounding the ingenuity that young people from immigrant communities and/or communities of color have within and across contexts. Taylor's commitment to care as a design value for digitally mediated learning interventions has been fundamentally shaped by her roles as mother, daughter, educator, and writer. Funded by, among others, the National Science Foundation, the NAEd/Spencer Foundation, and the Heising-Simons Foundation, her research and public scholarship can be found in venues such as *The Conversation*; the *Journal of the Learning Sciences, Cognition & Instruction*; *Connected Science Learning*; and *Learning, Media, & Technology*.

Nicholas J. Horton (*Planning Committee Co-Chair*, he/him/his) is Beitzel Professor of Technology and Society (statistics and data science) at Amherst College. He is passionate about improving quantitative and computational literacy for students with a variety of backgrounds and has worked to deepen engagement and mastery of higher-level concepts and data acumen. As an applied biostatistician, Horton's work is based within the mathematical and computational sciences but also spans other fields in order to ensure that research is conducted on a sound footing. The real-world research problems that these investigators face often require the use of novel solutions and approaches, since existing methodology is sometimes inadequate. Bridging the gap between theory and practice in interdisciplinary settings is often a challenge and has been a particular focus of Horton's work in missing data methods and longitudinal regression. He served as the chair of the Committee of Presidents of Statistical Societies, as a member of the Roundtable on Data Science Postsecondary Education, and as a member of the National Academies of Sciences, Engineering, and Medicine's Data Science for Undergraduates Consensus Study, and he is a co-chair of the National Academies' Committee on Applied and Theoretical Statistics. Horton has published a plethora of papers in statistics and biomedical research and four books on statistical computing and data science. He has been the recipient of several teaching awards and the American Statistical Association Founders Award. Horton is a fellow of the American Statistical Association and the American Association for the Advancement of Science. He earned his A.B. from Harvard College and his Sc.D. in biostatistics from the Harvard School of Public Health.

Ryan "Seth" Jones (*Presenter*, he/him/his) studies ways of supporting students to use mathematics and science to construct and revise knowledge. He has conducted research that focuses on measuring the extent to which whole class discussions in middle grades classrooms support students to examine the epistemological implications of various statistical properties, worked on interdisciplinary teams to create innovative technologies for teachers and students in middle grades math, helped to develop new tools for assessing nuanced ways of thinking in middle grades, and has developed frameworks and curricular approaches for interdisciplinary STEM learning environments organized around data modeling practices. Jones is currently leading a team funded by a National Science Foundation CAREER Award that is working to help middle school math and science teachers better coordinate their instruction around data and statistics so that students can have a more coherent learning experience.

Randy Kochevar (*Presenter*, he/him/his) is director of the Oceans of Data Institute at the Education Development Center Inc. (EDC), where he oversees a portfolio of projects to build data literacy skills in K–16 students and to help build pathways for data science and analytics careers. In addition to his role at EDC, Kochevar teaches environmental science and environmental science lab at Monterey Peninsula College. He trained as a deep-sea biologist at the University of California, Santa Barbara, studying the physiology of hydrothermal vent and hydrocarbon seep animals. The discovery of similar animal communities in the Monterey Submarine Canyon brought Kochevar up the coast, initially to the Monterey Bay Aquarium Research Institute and then to the Monterey Bay Aquarium, where he was involved in exhibit development, website development and print publishing, and media relations. He then worked at Stanford University's Hopkins Marine Station, collaborating with Barbara Block on electronic tagging of marine apex predators including tunas, billfish, and sharks.

Hollylynne Stohl Lee (*Planning Committee Member*, she/her/hers) is a distinguished professor of mathematics and statistics education in the Department of STEM Education at North Carolina State University, and a senior faculty fellow at the Friday Institute for Educational Innovation. She directs the Hub for Innovation and Research in Statistics Education at the Friday Institute. Lee's research focuses on teaching and learning of probability, statistics, and data science in grades 4–12 and early college. She is an expert on the design and use of technology tools to facilitate students' learning of mathematics and statistics, as well as in preparing preservice and in-service teachers to use technology. She is the recipient of the Robert Foster Cherry Award for Great Teaching from Baylor University and a fellow of the American Statistical Association, and has been awarded the University of North Carolina's Board of Governor's award for excellence in teaching. She designs and offers free online professional development for teachers, related to teaching statistics and data science, as well as creates and distributes open educational resources for preservice teacher education. Lee earned her Ph.D. from University of Virginia, M.A. Ed. from William & Mary, and B.S. from Pennsylvania State University.

Victor R. Lee (*Presenter*, he/him/his) is an associate professor in the Graduate School of Education at Stanford University. Through his research, he asks what STEM knowledge, tools, and practices are important to know in order to enable active participation and critical engagement with our increasingly digitally infused lives. Currently, this work involves researching and designing experiences for K–12 teaching and learning about data—often through a "quantified" self perspective, documenting and supporting the development of computational thinking in elementary school classrooms, and analyzing and supporting maker education in out-of-school settings. Lee has been past recipient of the National Science Foundation CAREER Award, the Jan Hawkins early career award from the American Educational Research Association, and a National Academy of Education/ Spencer Foundation Postdoctoral Fellowship, and he is a fellow of the International Society of the Learning Sciences. His work appears in leading national and international journals, and he was a co-author on the National Academies of Sciences, Engineering, and Medicine's consensus report *Cultivating Interest and Competencies for Computing*. Lee completed his undergraduate education in the areas of cognitive science, human-computer interaction, and mathematics at University of California, San Diego, and his Ph.D. in learning sciences at Northwestern University.

Anne Ottenbreit-Leftwich (*Presenter*, she/her/hers) is the Barbara B. Jacobs Chair in Education and Technology at Indiana University–Bloomington. She is also a professor and interim chair of instructional systems technology within the School of Education and an adjunct professor of computer science. Leftwich's expertise lies in the areas of the design of K–12 curriculum resources (particularly focused on technology and computer science), the use of technology to support teacher education, and the development/implementation of professional development for teachers and teacher educators. She investigates ways to teach computer science and ways to prepare preservice and inservice teachers to teach computer science. Leftwich is a co-principal investigator for the Expanding Computing Education Pathways Alliance, which seeks to broaden participation in computing at the K–16 levels. She is also a co-founder of CSforIN, which focuses on increasing computer science access opportunities for all K–12 Indiana students. Her research focuses on the adoption and implementation of technology and computer science at the K–12 levels.

Josephine Louie (*Presenter*, she/her/hers) is a senior research scientist and specializes in research on innovations in STEM education. Her research currently focuses on interventions that promote interests and learning in STEM fields of rapidly growing importance, such as data science, with an emphasis on collaborating with interdisciplinary teams and community partners to co-develop greater educational opportunities for learners from historically marginalized communities. Drawing on her extensive expertise in quantitative and qualitative research methodologies, Louie is the principal investigator of multiple projects funded by the National Science Foundation. She leads the Strengthening Data Literacy across the Curriculum project, which has been researching high school mathematics curriculum modules focused on social justice issues to promote understanding of and interests in statistics and data analysis among students from Black, Latinx, and low-income communities. She also leads the WeatherX: Understanding Weather Extremes with Big Data project, which has been developing and studying middle school science curriculum units to promote students' interests and abilities in data practices as they learn about extreme weather and long-term climate patterns in their local communities. She has published on research-practice partnerships in STEM education, the impacts of professional learning for mathematics teachers of English learners, and research methods in evaluating STEM education interventions. She received an A.B. in social studies from Harvard College, an M.C.P. from the Massachusetts Institute of Technology, and an Ed.D. from the Harvard Graduate School of Education.

Suyen Machado (*Presenter*, she/her/hers) is the data science education project director at the University of California, Los Angeles. She is a former classroom teacher, instructional coach, professional development facilitator, and administrator for the Los Angeles Unified School District (LAUSD). Machado is co-author of the Introduction to Data Science (IDS) curriculum, a high school data science course that authentically engages students in working with and reasoning critically about data in all forms. The IDS curriculum, originally piloted at LAUSD, is being implemented nationally and internationally. In addition to co-authoring IDS, she leads the team that designed and developed the IDS professional development series. Machado's work focuses on developing STEM curricula that engage students and improve teachers' pedagogical skills. Her ultimate goal is to bring 21st century data science teaching and learning to K–12 education.

Camillia Matuk (*Planning Committee Member*, she/her/hers) is assistant professor in New York University's Steinhardt's Educational Communication and Technology program, and director of RIDDLE. She serves as an associate editor for *Instructional Science*, a member of the editorial board of the *International Journal for Computer Supported Collaborative Learning*, and a member of the Education Committee for the International Society for the Learning Sciences. Matuk is also co-chair of the C2 ICCE Computer-Supported Collaborative Learning and Learning Sciences, a subconference of the International Conference for Computers in Education, of the Asia-Pacific Society for Computers in Education. Her research examines the design of interdisciplinary STEM learning experiences, with a focus on exploring how arts-based inquiry can promote K–16 learners' research and data literacies. Matuk received her Ph.D. in learning sciences from Northwestern University and was a postdoc at the Graduate School of Education at the University of California, Berkeley.

Stephanie Melville (*Presenter*, she/her/hers) strives to bring dynamic change to UTK–12 education as a central office math coach with the San Diego Unified School District. She began the Data Science Initiative in the San Diego Unified School District by increasing access to relevant and rigorous STEM courses, providing flexible pathways to graduation, and paving the way for future pathways as industry demands. Her greatest hope is to see equitable education policy put into place that makes data science a non-negotiable part of curricula, allowing historically excluded populations to gain entry to fields in which their voices are desperately needed.

Gemma F. Mojica (*Presenter*, she/her/hers) is a research scholar at the Friday Institute at North Carolina State University, where she focuses on the teaching and learning of statistics and data science. She has over a decade of experience designing, implementing, and researching various models of professional learning in small settings and at scale, which includes designing and implementing online curricular materials, technology tools, and online learning platforms for teachers. Mojica works on the Hub for Innovation and Research in Statistics Education team on multiple initiatives focused on building foundations for K–12 data science education and data-informed citizenry.

Leigh F. Peake (*Planning Committee Member*, she/her/hers) joined the Gulf of Maine Research Institute (GMRI) as chief education officer, leading GMRI's extensive work with K–12 teachers and students across Maine in order to nurture scientific literacy in the next generation of Mainers. She is a seasoned educational publishing executive and entrepreneur who came to GMRI from Education Development Center (EDC) in Waltham, MA, where she was director of New Enterprise Initiatives. Prior to EDC, Peake served as president of Corwin and senior vice president of SAGE Publications in California. She also spent a considerable time at Heinemann Publishing in Portsmouth, NH, where she directed the work of 10 editors in the development of one of the premier lines of professional resources and services for teachers. Peake is principal investigator of numerous National Science Foundation awards that research the affordances of informal learning experience in building data literacy in the context of investigations of climate change. She is also a principal investigator on a National Aeronautics and Space Administration Science Activation project, which aims to leverage a learning ecosystem framework to enable teachers, librarians, and informal educators to collaborate on climate/data learning experiences for youth. Finally, as a member of the chair teams for three years of the Gordon Research Conference on Visualization in Science and Education, Peake has had the opportunity to learn from a wide interdisciplinary network of experts who constantly push her practice with, and ambitions for, youth and educators.

Leticia Perez (*Presenter*, she/her/hers) is a former high school integrated and Advanced Placement program environmental science teacher with a passion for creating opportunities for educators to explore the intersections of identity, data, computational thinking, and rightful presence within STEM classrooms. Currently, she is applying lessons learned from working with the GAISE II team to support the development of data fluency professional learning modules and frameworks at WestEd. Perez's previous work includes developing and supporting teachers with K–12 science storylines, lesson study, and supporting teacher leader cohorts with the University of California, Los Angeles Science Project. There, she also served as the curriculum director for STEM+C3, which focuses on integrating computational thinking and data literacy within its teacher education program.

Josh Radinsky (*Presenter*, he/him/his) is an associate professor of learning sciences and education at the University of Illinois at Chicago. His research examines sensemaking with data in middle school, high school, and college classrooms; everyday data practices; and the design of data visualization tools, curriculum, and instruction. Radinsky teaches courses on the design of learning environments, qualitative research methods, and social studies teaching methods, among others, and does professional development with middle school and high school social studies teachers. He is former co-editor in chief of the *Journal of the Learning Sciences*, and a fellow of the International Society of the Learning Sciences.

Josh Recio (*Presenter*, he/him/his) is a member of the curriculum team at the Charles A. Dana Center, where he authors and manages content development for Agile Mind middle and high school mathematics course programs. Recio also supports the Dana Center's Launch Years Initiative, which seeks to usher in a new paradigm to support students for college preparation and guide them through mathematics pathways for degree attainment, specifically focusing on the transition from the junior year of high school through the junior year in college.

Joshua M. Rosenberg (*Presenter*, he/him/his) is an assistant professor of STEM education and faculty fellow at the Center for Enhancing Education in Mathematics and Sciences at the University of Tennessee, Knoxville. His research focuses on how learners think of and with data, particularly in science education settings. A former high school science teacher, Rosenberg tries to understand how practices such as creating, representing, and modeling data create new opportunities for learning how to use data to pose and answer questions about scientific phenomena. In addition to how learners think of and with data, he is also interested in student engagement across a range of STEM learning environments and the use of technology in education, particularly for teacher professional development. As a part of this work, Rosenberg makes use of quantitative methods, such as multilevel models and their Bayesian extensions for analyzing data collected through the experience sampling method, and newer approaches, such as social network analysis to analyze teachers' conversations on social media. He has been awarded generously in federal grants as principal investigator or co-principal investigator and has published in outlets such as *Journal of Research in Science Teaching*, *AERA Open*, and *Educational Researcher*. He received his Ph.D. from Michigan State University.

Andee Rubin (*Presenter*, she/her/hers) is a mathematician, computer scientist, and learning scientist at TERC, an educational research and development non-profit, where she has been studying the growth of students' and teachers' statistical reasoning, particularly as it is enabled by research-based tools for statistics education. She was involved in the development of several such pieces of software—Stretchy Histograms, Shifty Lines, TinkerPlots, and Fathom—and led the ViSOR (Visualizing Statistical Reasoning) project, which studied how middle and high school teachers used data visualization tools with their students. Rubin has developed curriculum materials around data for students as young as six, both in and out of school, as well as professional development materials for teachers and out-of-school facilitators. She was principal investigator of the Data Clubs project, which developed three data modules for middle school students in informal contexts. Rubin is currently principal investigator of four projects creating materials to facilitate students' learning about data and doing research on students' successes and struggles as they explore large and complex datasets. She is committed to empowering all learners to use data to pursue social justice.

Rafi Santo (*Presenter*, he/him/his) is a learning scientist focused on the intersection of digital culture, education, and institutional change. As principal researcher at Telos Learning, he partners with education institutions, foundations, coalitions, and government agencies to generate insights through basic and applied research, develop novel strategies for impact, and create new designs for equitable learning. Santo has studied, collaborated with, and facilitated a range of organizational networks related to digital learning, computing, and technology in education including the Mozilla Hive NYC Learning Network, CSforALL, the National Aeronautics and Space Administration, and the Corporation for Public Broadcasting. His scholarship spans multiple levels of activity—from understanding youth learning pathways across settings to investigating policy implementation and organizational network design—in order to develop practical insights that come from a holistic perspective. Santo's work has been supported by the Spencer Foundation, the MacArthur Foundation, the Wallace Foundation, the National Science Foundation, the Mozilla Foundation, the Susan Crown Exchange, Google, and the Corporation for Public Broadcasting. Santo holds a Ph.D. in learning and developmental sciences from Indiana University.

Emmanuel Schanzer (*Presenter*, he/him/his) is the co-founder of Bootstrap, which builds curricula that bring integrated computing to the mainstream classes that reach every child. He is an educational researcher and curriculum developer, as well as a former public school teacher from Boston and program manager at Microsoft. Schanzer is a longtime advocate for equity in education and is the director of National CSPdWeek. He holds degrees in computer science and education and completed his doctoral studies at Harvard with a research focus on using programming to teach algebra.

Heidi Schweingruber (*Presenter*, she/her/hers) is the director of the Board on Science Education at the National Academies of Sciences, Engineering, and Medicine. She oversees a portfolio of work that includes K–12 science education, informal science education, and higher education. Schweingruber initially joined the staff of the board as a senior program officer. In this role, she directed or co-directed several projects including the study that resulted in the report *A Framework for K–12 Science Education*, the blueprint for the Next Generation Science Standards. Schweingruber is a nationally recognized leader in leveraging research findings to catalyze improvements in science and STEM education policy and practice. She holds a Ph.D. in psychology (developmental) and anthropology from the University of Michigan.

Tricia Shelton (*Presenter*, she/her/hers) is chief learning officer at the National Science Teaching Association, supporting educators and students across the country as they work to integrate contemporary research in science education into classroom teaching and learning. She designs and leads professional learning, writes curriculum, speaks on panels, and works with national groups to promote science teaching and learning for all students as recommended by research and policy. Previously, Shelton was a middle and high school science teacher and teacher leader in Kentucky.

Lissa Soep (*Presenter*, she/her/hers) is special project producer and senior scholar-in-residence at YR Media, a youth-driven production company where she served as executive producer for journalism. She has produced and edited countless pieces of audio, online, and interactive features; helped establish YR Media's editorial standards; led research partnerships; launched the Teach YR initiative to scale learning beyond Oakland headquarters; and—with YR Media alum Asha Richardson—founded the country's first youth coding program embedded in a national newsroom. Soep's stories, co-created with youth and other colleagues, have won Peabody, Murrow, Kennedy, Investigative Reporters and Editors, Third Coast International Audio Festival, Gracie, and NLGJA awards. Investigative projects for which she's served on the senior team have advanced reforms in juvenile justice and child welfare. Her work as a writer, producer, and editor has been featured on NPR, NYT, CityLab, KQED, and Teen Vogue. Soep's books include *Code for What?* (forthcoming), *Participatory Politics, Drop that Knowledge,* and *Youthscapes*. She served on the Youth and Participatory Politics research network—a group of scholars brought together by the MacArthur Foundation to shift how we understand and promote youth civic life in digital times. Soep is an advisor to the Civic Imagination Project at the University of Southern California and the Data Literacy with, for, and by Youth project at Pratt Institute. She is a senior editor with the Vox Media Podcast Network and led development of learning tools for Vox Media's Language, Please initiative. Soep received her Ph.D. from Stanford University.

Alfred Spector (*Presenter*, he/him/his) is a visiting scholar at the Massachusetts Institute of Technology. His career began with innovation in large-scale, networked computing systems (at Stanford, as a professor at Carnegie Mellon University, and as founder of Transarc) and then transitioned to research leadership (as global vice president of IBM Software Research, Google Research, and then as chief technology officer of Two Sigma Investments). Spector has lectured widely on the growing importance of computer science across all disciplines ("CS+X"), and he has just completed co-authoring *Data Science in Context: Foundations, Challenges, and Opportunities*. He is a fellow of the the Association for Computing Machinery, IEEE, the National Academy of Engineering, and the American Academy of Arts and Sciences, where he serves on its council. Spector was a Hertz Fellow, won an IEEE Kanai Award for Distributed Computing, was co-awarded the ACM Software Systems Award, and was a Phi Beta Kappa Visiting Scholar. He received a Ph.D. from Stanford and an A.B. from Harvard.

Paul Strode (*Presenter*, he/him/his) teaches a hybrid Advanced Placement/International Baccalaureate biology course (grade 12), a one-semester anatomy and physiology crash course (grades 10–12), and a year-long science research seminar course (grades 10–12) at Fairview High School in Boulder, Colorado. Strode also teaches as an adjunct professor at the University of Colorado. He received the Evolution Education Award from the National Association of Biology Teachers (NABT) and later, he was selected by the

NABT as the Outstanding Biology Teacher for the Mountain Region. Strode is also a teaching ambassador for the Howard Hughes Medical Institute. He has a Ph.D. in ecology and environmental science from the University of Illinois, Urbana-Champaign, a masters in science education from the University of Washington, and a biochemistry degree from Manchester College (now University).

Stephen Miles Uzzo (*Presenter*, he/him/his) is chief scientist for the New York Hall of Science in New York City. He develops and leads large-scale design and research initiatives to study and integrate data-driven science into teaching and learning. His research interests include the coupling of complex human and natural systems, evolution and scaling of complex networks, equity and artificial intelligence, and the effect of climate change on vulnerable coastal communities. Uzzo holds a terminal degree in network theory and environmental studies from Union Institute and serves on a number of institutional and advisory boards related to his interests.

Michelle Hoda Wilkerson (*Planning Committee Co-Chair*, she/her/hers) is an associate professor in the Graduate School of Education and the Graduate Group in Science and Mathematics Education at the University of California, Berkeley. Wilkerson's research addresses the following question: How is computing changing what is important to teach and learn in grades 5–12 science and mathematics classes? This has led her to study how young people learn with and about scientific computing tools such as simulations, data analysis packages, and interactive visualizations. Most recently, Wilkerson's work has explored how learners' status as consumers, subjects, and creators of data shape what they understand and engage with during analysis. Her work has been supported by the National Science Foundation, the George Lucas Education Foundation, and Google Education Research. Wilkerson's work was awarded by an Early CAREER grant from the National Science Foundation and the American Educational Research Association's Jan Hawkins Award for Humanistic Research and Scholarship in Learning Technologies. She received her Ph.D. in learning sciences in 2012 from Northwestern University.

Trena Wilkerson (*Presenter*, she/her/hers) is president of the National Council of Teachers of Mathematics, an international mathematics education organization with more than 30,000 members. She is also professor of mathematics education in the Department of Curriculum and Instruction in the School of Education at Baylor University and interim department chair. Wilkerson teaches both graduate and undergraduate mathematics education courses and conducts professional development and research. She previously taught high school mathematics. Wilkerson received the Award for Excellence in Integrating Science and Mathematics from the School Science Mathematics Association for her role as director of the GEAR UP Math Initiative funded by the U.S. Department of Education. She has received the Prakken Professional Cooperation Award from the International Technology and Engineering Educators Association, the Association of Mathematics Teacher Education-Texas Outstanding Service Award, and the Texas Council of Teachers of Mathematics E. Glenadine Gibb Achievement Award for her contribution to the improvement of mathematics education at the state and national levels. Wilkerson's research interests include mathematics education, algebra teacher efficacy, and professional development. She has published in numerous research and practitioner journals and has presented at numerous state, national, and international conferences.

Appendix C

Submitted Cases

Workshop registrants were invited to submit case examples on K–12 data science education for one of three topic areas:

Examples of challenges educators face when working to enact data science activities;

Examples that reflect successful real-world application of data science with youth; or

Examples of an existing software/tool/technology that has been used and could be adopted to supplement data science learning.

Cases were featured during the workshop. A summary of the cases can be found in Table C-1.[1]

[1]The full cases are available at https://www.nationalacademies.org/event/09-13-2022/docs/DC43B789C2136F62C030FAE3E7A8EB58C45EF823FACF

TABLE C-1 Submitted Cases by Case Type

Case Type: Challenges Educators Face		
Case Title	*Description*	*Relevant Links/Citations*
Access to Data Science Courses in K–12	Data science courses are not widely taught at the high school level. Partnerships between colleges, nonprofits, and high schools will need to be established to support, implement, and sustain high-quality professional development, and course development. What are examples of successful partnerships to facilitate data science teaching and learning at the K–12 levels?	
Lack of Data Science Fundamentals	Learning the fundamentals of how data are collected, analyzed, and communicated starts with a solid foundation in the science and engineering practices outlined in the *Framework for Science Education*. One challenge educators face when teaching data science is the lack of fundamentals. Connecting an abstract concept like data science to real-world applications can be a huge barrier when it comes to keeping students engaged. Many science teachers struggle to engage students actively and feel stuck using slides, lectures, and traditional science experiments to collect data that can be time-consuming to set up and maintain. Teachers need time to be teachers, and students feel more engaged when they connect data to the world in which they live.	
Gulf of Maine Research Institute	Inquiry-, interest-, and place-based pedagogies typically are described as highly engaging for learners whether in the classroom or in an informal learning context like 4-H. Yet these approaches pose challenges to learners having a data-rich experience. Data relevant to explorations of my place or my question can be difficult to secure, too complicated for the developmental stage of the learner, or simply may not exist. Where it exists, data provenance may not be obvious and may therefore hide important information from the novice data scientist. This produces what we call "data dead ends" and frustration—	

	independent learners design interesting questions to pursue but become exhausted at the task of finding and accessing data that might inform their investigations. Where data exist and are usable, many tools don't support authentic work with the data by novices.
Gulf of Maine Research Institute	In response to dramatic media reports about massive die-offs of moose, a class in Aroostook, ME, decides to investigate the impact of ticks on Maine moose populations and its link to climate change. They need to secure and visualize state data on both tick and moose populations alongside precipitation and temperature data over a long enough period to distinguish a climate-driven trend from an anomalous year/period or natural variability. Tick populations also turn out to be related to several key invasive plant species (e.g., barberry) that are tick "magnets." Ideally, they would do so in a tool that allows them to mess around with the data in an inquiry-based fashion. And, like most climate phenomena, they need a tool that allows them to view change over both space and time.
Need for High-Quality, Consistent Data Science Training for Practitioners	Regardless of how hard we work at designing clear, important, and meaningful district and state science and math standards and guidelines that incorporate data science skill development, what actually ends up happening in the classroom may be vastly different than our intentions. The amount of training on data science that K–12 teachers have and their confidence with teaching it has immense variability, even within a single school, mine included. Many teachers thus either avoid doing much meaningful data science with their students or they transfer their own misunderstandings onto their students by doing it wrong.

continued

TABLE C-1 Continued

Case Type: Challenges Educators Face		
Case Title	*Description*	*Relevant Links/Citations*
Differences Between Data Science and Statistics—Need for High-Quality, Consistent Data Science Training for Practitioners	Many educators don't receive great training on how to implement a data science curriculum, so they fall back on old practices and rely on their knowledge of statistics to push them through. This usually leads to students being in courses labeled as data science but taught as statistics, which is to say they omit the computer science aspects that are so necessary to the implementation of a data science foundation. To this point, many math educators don't think they belong in the computer science field (many also don't believe they belong in the statistics field, strangely). However, in California, you need a math credential to teach computer science, so the disconnect is probably as a result of their preservice courses (many of which lack a computer science strand).	
Lack of Time, Physical Resources, and Staff Are a Hurdle for Many Implementing Data Science Courses	My colleagues and I led a statewide professional development course—"What Is Data Science?"—for high school math teachers last year. During this course the teachers identified challenges they face when working to incorporate data science activities. Some of these challenges included time restraints—including the excessive number of math standards they are expected to cover; scheduling restraints—many teachers in Idaho teach in rural schools where there is often only one or two high school math teachers for the entire school; the infeasibility of adding in a full data science class; their own fear or lack of time to learn a new software/tool/technology in order to teach data science—we are thinking as a state to offer a follow-up professional development course that is intentionally designed to help 6–12 educators get over this hurdle; and explicit connections between data science and mathematics content standards—many math teachers want to know they are still teaching math when they are leading data science activities.	

Use of Excel vs. SPSS for Data Analysis	In science education research, students usually analyze data using the Excel program; because of the advantages of this program, students can detect and design the data analysis formulas used. However, when using SPSS, students can only output but do not know how to process data analysis in SPSS. This is an obstacle that is often faced by students when the results of the analysis are presented, where they are not able to explain how the data analysis process is carried out. As an answer to these problems, I often suggest to students that before using SPSS, first read the SPSS Manual to get an in-depth picture of the contents of the SPSS program, especially related to the use of statistical formulas in SPSS.
Difficulties Finding Clean, Multivariate Datasets	With regard to teaching science, it is very challenging to find relatively clean, multivariate datasets that allow for rich exploration of science topics that are directly relevant to what teachers are currently teaching. That is, in order to incorporate data science into an already over-full, year-long curriculum, teachers need to access multivariate datasets that will enable their students to learn the science by working with the data. Such datasets are difficult to find and take a lot of digging to find—even when they exist.

continued

TABLE C-1 Continued

Case Type: Challenges Educators Face

Case Title	*Description*	*Relevant Links/Citations*
Judging in K–12 Science and Engineering Fairs	Judges in K–12 science and engineering fairs often find students have very poor grasps of basic statistics and probability, and nearly zero comprehension of error sources and variability. We cannot leave statistics to a high school AP statistics course! Data science basics need to include the basics of these important mathematical concepts, and teachers need support to do that inclusion. More data are NOT equal to better data, necessarily; evaluating data quality is similar in concept to evaluating bibliographic sources.	
Enhancing Statistics Teacher Education through E-Modules [ESTEEM] (NSF DUE 1625713)	The ESTEEM project began in 2016 to develop teacher education curriculum materials designed to support secondary (grades 6–12) mathematics teachers to learn to teach statistics. The project's focus on the statistical education of teachers was due to increased expectations for students to learn statistics at the secondary level that needed to be matched by enhancement and prioritization of statistics teacher education. The ESTEEM project packages materials into e-modules. Their modular format makes their use more flexible for faculty, allowing them to choose the modules that work best in their teacher preparation program. The modules are easily imported into learning management systems [LMSs] for adaptation and integration with other course materials. Faculty can access the entire set of ESTEEM-developed modules at the ESTEEM portal, available through free registration. At the ESTEEM portal, faculty can download a version of the complete set of materials in an easy-to-use format that can be imported into Canvas, Moodle, or Blackboard. We also offer a Common Cartridge format that can be imported into other LMSs. All materials are distributed using the Creative Commons Attribution Noncommercial Share-Alike 4.0 license.	http://go.ncsu.edu/esteem https://www.fi.ncsu.edu/projects/esteem

Implementing Data Science Outside of Mathematics Curriculum	Data science is interdisciplinary in nature. However, the core curriculum places most of the work in developing students' understanding of data within mathematics. In taking this approach, mathematical techniques tend to get foregrounded, and other aspects of critical data literacy remain underdeveloped. To better prepare students as citizens in an increasingly data-driven world, we need students to have opportunities to engage with data across the curriculum. This raises the challenge of better understanding how data science education intersects with subject matter taught across the curriculum, the pedagogical content knowledge teachers from different disciplines draw upon as they integrate data investigations with existing curricula, and the resources teachers need to do this.
Hesitation in Students Surrounding Data Science	Data science is so new that students do not have a fundamental understanding of what it is, or even who uses it, which makes diving into the curriculum difficult. Students also have a false sense of the education that is necessary to pursue a career in a data field because they are under the false assumption that anything that is in math must require a college education and a great deal of higher math, which scares students and creates hesitation around the field. I began my year with two activities during the first week of school: Introduction to Data Literacy Skills: Students worked in groups to learn about a skill and made a mini-poster explaining the skill in their own words. Students had an immediate introduction to what data science and data literacy are though this activity and were able to easily transition into the curriculum with a basic background of what this class would cover. Career Project: Student pairs chose a career to research that uses data science and were asked to find information about that career, including education requirements and average salary. Students then presented their findings to their peers. The results were very positive. Students realized from the first week of school that there are careers they never heard of that are in high demand right now that don't require extensive education after high school. Students became excited about the possibility of opening up new future opportunities. Share-Alike 4.0 license.

continued

TABLE C-1 Continued

Case Type: Challenges Educators Face		
Case Title	*Description*	*Relevant Links/Citations*
Using Data to Answer Questions That Are Important to Students	One goal (an important one, in my opinion) in data science education is for students to pose investigative questions that are important to them and to use data to answer (at least partially) their questions. This poses big challenges to the instructor, who must potentially grade or assess many different projects, and must have sufficient confidence in their own knowledge of data analysis to assist students to follow many different pathways, without knowing ahead of time what the "right" answer is. Even when working with the same dataset, different students might pursue different approaches. How do we prepare instructors so that they can support students to follow valid approaches without teaching the misconception that "you can say anything with data"?	
EDC's Oceans of Data Institute	The Education Development Center's (EDC's) Oceans of Data Institute has explored how educators can integrate the use of authentic data into their teaching practice. Topic areas include Earth science, biology, social studies, and civil engineering. In all cases, students work with "CLIP" data, which are complex, large, interactively accessed using a computer, and professionally collected. This approach models real-world situations and helps to build critical "habits of mind" when analyzing and interpreting the data. One of the recurring challenges in having students work with CLIP data has to do with the nature of the interface itself, which typically has to do three things simultaneously. Allow students to explore and manipulate the data in various forms, including tables, graphs, and maps; Allow space for written instructions, prompts, or background; and Give students a way to capture their work—ideally in such a way that the instructor can review it and provide feedback.	https://edc.org/oceans-data-institute

	Previous solutions have included the following: Use of a bespoke Web-based interface and Concord Consortium's CODAP interface. Use of Concord's LARA framework, which easily integrates either CODAP or SageModeler interactive data windows. Integration of CODAP and SageModeler data windows into Canvas. Canvas would allow integrations of these tools into a single page, but website navigation takes up much of the screen real estate. Early feedback from undergraduate students suggests that they are comfortable navigating multiple tabs/windows to work around this issue; they are uncertain how younger students will respond to this workaround.
EMBEDS: Exploring the Mathematics of Biological Ecosystems with Data Science	The EMBEDS project at TERC and the University of Colorado, Boulder is integrating "data excursions" into a ninth-grade biology unit on the changing ecology of the Serengeti by using the same datasets scientists used to understand why the populations of both wildebeest and buffalo increased rapidly and substantially between 1960 and 1975. Challenges: Scientific datasets from several decades ago are not always available and require a lot of work to make them usable by current-day students. Difficulties in techniques for measuring ecological quantities. Students hypothesized that an increased food source could drive population growth, but we were uncertain how to measure the food supply in the Serengeti—an issue scientists also had—so we used rainfall as a proxy. Data indicated that rainfall did not increase during the period of population growth, urging the students to draw a conclusion contradictory to their hypothesis and two challenges arose:

continued

TABLE C-1 Continued

Case Type: Challenges Educators Face		
Case Title	*Description*	*Relevant Links/Citations*
	Understanding how data can indicate NO relationship between two variables, and Reasoning about food availability through the proxy quantity of rainfall. These challenges arose because we were trying to fulfill two different learning goals: Introduce the basics of data science, and Embed science concepts dictated by the NGSS. NGSS suggests that students in ninth grade use mathematical and computational models in science, but simultaneously teaching science and data fluency is not straightforward because students may lack the skills they need to do this effectively. Our students struggled with covariation, so we developed materials to introduce basic graph analysis and relevant scientific principles.	https://www.nsf.gov/awardsearch/showAward?AWD_ID=2031459&HistoricalAwards=false
Incorporating "Messy" Datasets into Classroom Instruction	Teachers (at all educational levels, K–16) often struggle to incorporate real-world, complex, "messy" datasets into classroom instructional activities—even when those data are easily available in online sources, like interactive data maps or news features. Students easily navigate to confusing and complicated places in those data sources, and a teacher can be utterly lost when coming around to help them.	

InquirySpace	The National Science Foundation (NSF)-funded InquirySpace projects, aimed at providing opportunities for helping youth engage in independent STEM investigations, represent a successful real-world application of data science. Aspects of the curriculum provide enlightening opportunities that other programs may be able to adopt or emulate. One specific set of examples derives from classroom observations in the project that showed students leveraging graphs as epistemic tools. Video analysis of extended classroom interactions indicated that student use of data graphs during sensor-based experiments could range from a focus on producing them as a procedural display to engaging deeply over several days to make sense of different graphical representations of their data. In a multi-case study, we investigated high school physics students' use of graphs and what prompted those uses. Unexpected data patterns and graphical anomalies appeared to play a strong role in provoking student reasoning and triggering engagement with the graphs. For the three representative groups subject to in-depth analysis, graphs appeared to play an important role in their knowledge production as they made decisions about their experimental procedures and goodness of data. We conclude that when students produce data in an experiment for which they feel a sense of ownership, they can exhibit an almost proprietary interest in representations of their data. As they work to create alignments between their conceptions of their data and the unexpected data patterns they see in the graphs, they begin to use their graphs as epistemic tools.	https://concord.org/our-work/research-projects/inquiryspace/

continued

TABLE C-1 Continued

Case Type: Existing Tool/Software/Technology

Case Title	*Description*	*Relevant Links/Citations*
Gulf of Maine Research Institute	Our work focuses on explorations of locally relevant impacts of climate change. At its heart, climate change is change over both space and time. Our experience is that existing tools do one or the other well but not both. So CODAP is fantastic for time series data. Tools from Esri and Field Scope are great for geographic information system (GIS) data. This is complicated by pedagogy. CODAP is designed for a "messing around" approach to working with data, which we love. To our knowledge there's no equivalent that allows play with GIS, particularly over time. Animation of place over time is the likely current solution but I don't THINK (could be wrong!) any existing tools put that power in the hands of learners.	https://gmri.org/
CourseKata	CourseKata Statistics and Data Science, an innovative interactive online textbook for teaching introductory statistics and data science in colleges, universities, and high schools. Part of CourseKata's Better Book Project is to leverage research and student data to guide continuous improvement of online learning resources.	https://coursekata.org
STATS4STEM	Fully funded by the National Science Foundation, STATS4STEM provides a collection of learning, assessment, tutoring, data, and computing resources for statistics educators and their students. Our assessment and tutoring feature allows for instantaneous student feedback with question-specific hints for students who are struggling. In addition, real-time learning charts and reports are available to help educators adapt instruction to meet the individual needs of their students. Our computing resources integrate real-world data with the RStudio statistical computing platform, allowing all students the opportunity to conduct real-world statistical analysis. Finally, in an effort to foster community, our site integrates a message board for statistics educators looking to share ideas, tips, and insights with other educators worldwide.	https://www.stats4stem.org/

	Any high school, college, or university educator worldwide who teaches statistics, or a course related to statistics, can register.	
Pivot Interactives	Two educators from Minneapolis, Minnesota, created a platform called Pivot Interactives that allows students to explore scientific phenomena and make sense of them through data analysis tools. Their goal is to ignite students' passion for science, and teachers' love for teaching, and to instill the proper fundamentals of collecting and analyzing data. Pivot Interactives is the only platform for interactive video-based science activities with embedded data-collection tools. Based on real-world science phenomena, students become engaged with data capture, process, analysis, and communication—the fundamentals of data science. Under controlled conditions, students who use a curriculum based on Pivot Interactives interactive video showed more significant learning gains in critical thinking skills even when compared to integrated hands-on learning. Science education researchers at the Massachusetts Institute of Technology (MIT) and Carleton College measured students' experience using Pivot Interactives interactive video compared to traditional methods: 85% reported that interactive video made it easier to understand the scenario being investigated, 92% said they'd encourage their friends to take courses that use interactive video, 65% wished MIT's online physics course included more of our interactive video, and 60% reported an increase in using scientific skills like measurement techniques when using our interactive video.	https://www.pivotinteractives.com/
Khan Lab School	I piloted a year-long data science course to high schoolers (fresh-seniors) last year and it went great! We used the CourseKata curriculum and supplemented with projects and other activities I created. We use Jupyter Notebooks along with an integrated textbook and Deepnote.com and R to analyze our data.	https://khanlabschool.org/

continued

TABLE C-1 Continued

Case Type: Existing Tool/Software/Technology		
Case Title	*Description*	*Relevant Links/Citations*
The FieldScope Project	FieldScope is an innovative map-based data collection and analysis platform managed by BSCS Science Learning. It supports citizen and community science projects and other initiatives with tools to collect data from dispersed geographic locations and to analyze trends, patterns, and change over time, including the impact of interventions. FieldScope enables organizations, community members, and learners to monitor and actively address issues, such as environmental and social challenges, that are concerning to them. It empowers participants in projects to use maps, graphs, and other visualization tools to make meaning of crowd-sourced datasets and turn data into stories that can be used in science communication and grassroots advocacy.	https://www.fieldscope.org
Invitations to Inquiry	Invitations to Inquiry are short instructional activities designed to help middle and high school students work with large data sets hosted on FieldScope. Teachers and students use the interactive FieldScope platform to collect, visualize, and analyze environmental data. With these new Inquiries, students can explore FieldScope's advanced mapping and graphing tools to dig deeper into data in the context of meaningful science classroom lessons. Each lesson engages students in interpreting graphs or maps, or both, and figuring out what the data mean. Ultimately, the Inquiries are intended to increase student confidence in working with data and using visualization tools. These Inquiries are designed for two to four days of learning and support the Science and Engineering Practices from the NGSS. They include teacher guides, slides, handouts, and other instructional resources and supports.	https://bscs.org/resources/invitations-to-inquiry/
Center for Curriculum Redesign (CCR)	My center has deeply redesigned math standards, in partnership with the Organisation for Economic Co-operation and Development, to reflect a K–12 emphasis on data science (aka stats/probs) and discrete/computational math.	https://curriculumredesign.org/modern-mathematics/

Data Nuggets	Data Nuggets are free classroom activities that bring authentic data and science stories into the classroom. More than 100 Data Nuggets are available on our website. Written by the scientists behind the research, each activity guides students through the process of working with a dataset to answer a scientific question. Because the authenticity of the research process is maintained, students often face unexpected results, messy data, and findings that do not support original hypotheses. Students who use Data Nuggets show increased interest in STEM careers, confidence when working with data, and improved abilities to construct scientific explanations.	https://datanuggets.org
DataClassroom and DataClassroom U	DataClassroom and DataClassroom U are web-apps for graphing, statistics, and data analysis in grades 6–12 and university level science and math classrooms. The tool runs on any device that can access the Internet and can integrate with LMSs such as Schoology, Clever, Google Classroom, Canvas, and Classlink. The tool has been designed by teachers to provide the opportunity to integrate next-generation data skills seamlessly with the learning experiences they are already creating. Functionally, students can produce a wide variety of data visualizations, and get support with graph choice, applying inferential statistics, and learning the math behind statistical tests with animation. The DataClassroom U version of the tool contains a Bridge to R which generates well annotated R code for any of the graphs or statistical tests called through the easy to use interface. This supports students early in the process of learning a statistical programming language. The app contains 100+ curated datasets and lessons that are available with the free version of the app.	https://about.dataclassroom.com/ https://u.dataclassroom.com/

continued

TABLE C-1 Continued

Case Type: Existing Tool/Software/Technology		
Case Title	*Description*	*Relevant Links/Citations*
Schoolytics	Schoolytics is a student data platform that gives data superpowers to teachers, administrators, parents, and students by building and automating data pipelines, and providing out-of-the-box data visualizations of academic data. We believe in empowering students with actionable data on their own progress and contend that students can and should have agency over their own learning. Schoolytics transforms Google Classroom assignment data into meaningful key performance indicators and time series trends for users to reflect on and respond to. By using their Schoolytics dashboard, students get exposure to simple statistics and graphs based on their own data, which takes on a personal and real quality that more theoretical discussions on data science struggle to match. In addition, because the primary source of data for Schoolytics is Google Classroom, teachers and students can engage together and work as partners in analyzing and interpreting the data.	https://www.schoolytics.com/
databot	databot™ is a company that is pretty passionate about K–12 data science. We sell a STEM device, databot™, a tiny, wireless, classroom-tough multi-sensor product with 15 built-in sensors. Students and educators can easily connect to databot™ via bluetooth and immediately have access to scientific data from databot™ including CO_2, volatile organic compounds, humidity, air pressure, and many more. databot™ joined the Data Science 4 Everyone coalition this summer and pledged to create 10 lesson plans that emphasize data science practices. The first is an air quality investigation.	https://databot.us.com/ds4e-iaq/

Helioviewer: A Solar Data Viewer from NASA	I would like to share an example of how a data tool can be designed and adapted for learners to enable students to better engage in analyzing and interpreting solar data and phenomena. A Solar Data Viewer from NASA, the Helioviewer was redesigned to put phenomena exploration first. Designing tools that better enable sensemaking and student exploration will be critical to the future of data science for learning.	https://helioviewer.org/ https://student.helioviewer.org/
Coding Like a Data Miner	We've developed an NSF-funded curriculum that teaches students how to scrape (i.e., data mine) Twitter along their personal interests. The curriculum combines quality computing practices and data science techniques using equity-driven framings. This means rather than navigate data sources generated by others, learners can construct their own data sources in real time. In this way, Coding Like a Data Miner is couched in real work applications suited to reflect the nature of the increasingly digital world around us!	https://www.nsf.gov/awardsearch/showAward?AWD_ID=2137708&HistoricalAwards=false
Ohio Data Science Foundations Course Pilot	This year I am involved in the Ohio Data Science Foundations Course Pilot: using the Data Science Curriculum (UCLA: Introduction to Data Science). By participating in this pilot I will be able to bring these two models together and finalize a course that is aligned with the state standards and provide my students with real-world engaging learning experience. Also, this year, two students from the Intro to Data Science from last semester are now enrolled in our apprenticeship class. The plan is they will prepare for the SAS certification test and explore options with local companies. Our school has just been approved to access the SAS Educator Portal; all Perry Lake students will be able to access the SAS Skill Builder for Students. These students will independently work through the SAS Virtual Learning Environment: SAS Programming 1: Essentials course to prepare them for the SAS certification. I believe these students will be the first in the state to add this credential to their resumes.	Information about course pilot: https://education.ohio.gov/Topics/Learning-in-Ohio/Mathematics/Resources-for-Mathematics/Math-Pathways/Data-Science-Foundations Referenced curriculum: https://www.idsucla.org/

continued

TABLE C-1 Continued

Case Type: Existing Tool/Software/Technology		
Case Title	*Description*	*Relevant Links/Citations*
University of Virginia School of Data Science	I have developed a high school level data science course with one of my students. The course launches this week at a private school in Charlottesville, VA. The course does two things: Students work together in small teams on an end-to-end data science project, which covers the Big Idea of a data science pipeline. Students select a project from an open-source repository of municipally generated data. Students learn the essential ingredients to accomplish they learn a mix of computing, data skills, modeling, and statistics.	
Awash in Data	Awash in Data is an always-evolving e-book by Tim Erickson introducing students (and teachers) to basic ideas in data science. It begins with a set of lessons that take about three hours of class time, plus homework and a mini-project. Students use CODAP throughout. The book itself is "live" in the sense that you can do many tasks in the book itself; that is, CODAP windows are embedded in the website. Like CODAP, the book is free and requires no sign-in to use. The introductory lessons have been used several times with high school students as a supplement to an applied math class. Erickson and Chen published an article describing the work. In 2020, Erickson used the book as the foundation for a one-semester high school introduction to data science. He is updating the book with assignments and learnings from that longer class.	https://www.concord.org/awashindata Erickson, T., and Chen, E. (2021). Introducing data science with data moves and CODAP. *Teaching Statistics, 43*(S1), S124–S132. https://onlinelibrary.wiley.com/doi/10.1111/test.12240
GAISE	Guidelines for Assessment and Instruction in Statistics Education (GAISE) Report: A Pre-K–12 Curriculum Framework provides recommendations and a curriculum framework with examples for teaching statistics in the pre-K–12 years.	Resources and information about GAISE: https://www.amstat.org/education/guidelines-for-assessment-and-instruction-in-statistics-education-(gaise)-reports

	I am putting GAISE in the "tool" category because learning needs to be assessed and the document provides direction for assessment. There are also many useful examples to help teachers see the path to integrating a data-centric approach while satisfying existing curricular demands.	
Friday Institute for Educational Innovation at North Carolina State University	When educators are ready to develop their skills in teaching data science and statistics, they can use online professional learning courses and platforms to engage with highly effective activities, videos, data investigations, readings, and assessments. Since 2015, 6,500+ educators from more than 90 countries have engaged in such self-guided learning through the Friday Institute for Educational Innovation at NC State University.	Two current self-paced professional learning opportunities include Amplifying Statistics and Data Science in Classrooms http://go.ncsu.edu/amplifystats InSTEP: Invigorating Statistics and Data Science Teaching Through Professional Learning http://instepwithdata.org
GAISE II	In 2020, *Pre-K–12 Guidelines for Assessment and Instruction in Statistics Education II (GAISE II): A Framework for Statistics and Data Science Education* was co-published by the American Statistical Association (ASA) and the National Council of Teachers of Mathematics (NCTM). GAISE II incorporates enhancements and new skills needed for making sense of data today while maintaining the spirit of the original Pre-K–12 GAISE report published in 2005.	Resources and information about GAISE: https://www.amstat.org/education/guidelines-for-assessment-and-instruction-in-statistics-education-(gaise)-reports
State Frameworks for Florida State	We have developed a four-course program of study for the Career and Technical Division for grades 9–12 and have it aligned to a draft version of the pending frameworks for the State/Community College Frameworks for Data Science and Fintech. We have started to develop an open-source curriculum portal in Canvas under a CC-Share Alike license for use by teachers. We provide professional development and coaching to teachers to help them develop the skills they need to successfully teach this course. We are creating data science projects with Florida themes in agriculture, health care, science, marine health, manufacturing, finance, and other career related areas working with industry partners for data sets. We can provide expanded versions of these frameworks.	See pages 62–70 for more information: https://www.nationalacademies.org/event/09-13-2022/docs/DC43B789C2136F62C030FAE3E7A8EB58C45EF823FACF

continued

TABLE C-1 Continued

Case Type: Existing Tool/Software/Technology

Case Title	*Description*	*Relevant Links/Citations*
WeatherX	WeatherX is an NSF-funded project that has been developing curriculum strategies to promote scientific data practices and interest in data science careers among middle school students in low-income rural areas. A major tool that WeatherX has developed is the National Oceanic and Atmospheric Administration (NOAA) Weather portal, a permanent plugin within the online data analysis and visualization tool CODAP. The portal provides anyone with a web browser access to large-scale weather data from NOAA. Using the portal, individuals can select and download hourly, daily, and monthly weather measurements (such as for temperature, wind speed, and precipitation levels) from 1,783 weather stations in the United States, with records spanning as far back as the mid-1800 to the present. Students using WeatherX lessons investigate data from their own local weather stations and make claims about whether specific weather events are extreme by comparing event data with 30-year climate averages. Based on research during an initial implementation of the WeatherX units, students and teachers spoke positively of the ability to investigate and learn from large-scale weather data from their own and other locations using the NOAA Weather portal and CODAP. In addition, teachers observed, and students reported, higher levels of confidence in making and interpreting graphs in CODAP after engaging in WeatherX activities. We will be making our WeatherX units available for public use in the upcoming months.	An online tutorial on how to make graphs in CODAP to examine weather data is available at https://codap.concord.org/app/static/dg/en/cert/index.html#shared=https://cfm-shared.concord.org/vljl6HALM3KwxorhbOEV/file.json
Jupyter Notebooks	Educationally designed Jupyter Notebooks based on Python make complex machine learning algorithms accessible and transparent to students. Jupyter Notebooks can be designed with a kind of menu-driven interface, where coding and recoding parts can be used, but that is not necessary. Jupyter Notebooks can be designed as worked examples that can scaffold students in writing a computational essay for their own data analysis. A computational essay can be conceived as in interactive changeable book with code, graphs, tables, and text that make a data analysis reproducible.	Fleischer, Y., Biehler, R., and Schulte, C. (2022). Teaching and learning data-driven machine learning with educationally designed Jupyter Notebooks. *Statistics Education Research Journal*, *21*(2). https://doi.org/10.52041/serj.v21i2.61

SocialExplorer	The website SocialExplorer, developed by sociologist Andrew Beveridge, is an excellent U.S. Census Data access tool. It is useful for researchers, teachers, students, and the public. The subscription version provides access to historical census data back to 1790, and the free public version has great mapping and reporting tools for recent censuses.	https://www.socialexplorer.com/
DataFlow	DataFlow is a comprehensive open-source platform for programming, data processing, and real-time data graphing. Within DataFlow, students can produce meaningful data and control the data through their lifecycle, making decisions as data flow from the collection device to a representation on screen. Students choose what data are being collected, where to collect them, how to modify or transform them, how to use the data to actuate a relay, how to store those data, and how to view the data.	For an example of DataFlow use: https://concord.org/newsletter/2020-spring/sensors-and-spinach-increasing-student-agency-in-biology-class/
	When working with real-world data, teachers and curriculum developers face many dilemmas. One of the most prominent lies in the complexity of these datasets. For example, some relevant datasets in ongoing projects may include tens of thousands of cases and over one hundred attributes. These datasets on their own are much too large and complicated for the middle school audience the project targets. Choosy, a simple data tool designed to address this issue, could be adopted broadly to enhance data science curricula and approaches. Designed to enable the straightforward creation of simple datasets from complex ones, Choosy is implemented as a plugin to CODAP. By allowing teachers or curriculum developers to work with and easily select sub-portions of larger datasets, it enables classroom activities or curriculum units to involve a much wider range of datasets than otherwise possible. Choosy has a simple interface, with a tab for selecting the dataset, a tab for attributes, and a tab for tagging specific cases. Users proceed through these tabs, using a dropdown to select their desired dataset, a series of checkboxes to identify the attributes they desire to include, and a streamlined interface to select specific cases to set aside or delete. When they are satisfied with their choices (which can be monitored in a live readout reporting the number of attributes and cases currently selected), users can export the final simplified dataset for inclusion in their desired activity.	Information about Choosy plugin: https://concord.org/newsletter/2021-fall/under-the-hood-three-new-codap-plugins/

continued

TABLE C-1 Continued

Case Type: Existing Tool/Software/Technology		
Case Title	*Description*	*Relevant Links/Citations*
Transformers Plugin for CODAP	In using CODAP, students can easily make simple changes to datasets by dragging and dropping attributes and creating formulas. However, this streamlined interface can render more complex operations difficult or impossible at times. Additionally, changes to datasets must be performed individually and repeated by hand, making the application of a series of data moves on multiple datasets tedious or prone to error. The Transformers plugin for CODAP is a tool aimed at addressing this issue. Designed by the Bootstrap curriculum with the goal of featuring data moves more prominently in its curriculum resources that use CODAP, the plugin provides 30 different transformations for users to apply to datasets automatically. Among many other transformations, this set of built-in transformations makes it easier for students to filter and sort attributes and to measure, aggregate, and summarize data. Additionally, the tool enables a more programmatic, documented, and repeatable approach to data transformation within the CODAP environment. Users can save sets of transformations as miniature programs, coming back to them later or saving them as mini-tools for future use.	Information about Transformer plugin: https://concord.org/newsletter/2021-fall/under-the-hood-three-new-codap-plugins/
Signification Plugin for CODAP	Students often have issues facing complex datasets. However, a significant fraction of learners are blind or visually impaired, rendering traditional visual data analysis tools practically inaccessible. An experimental plugin for CODAP aims to begin to address both of these issues by making data "visible" through signification, the use of audio portrayals of data.	

	It includes an interface for selecting a sub-portion of a dataset and a play button that loops through the selected subset repeatedly. As it loops through the dataset, the plugin translates the data into audio signals, varying aspects of the audio including pitch, timbre, and other attributes. Users can assign different attributes of a dataset to different aspects of the audio output to allow for examination of multiple attributes simultaneously, modify the speed and repetition rate of the looping to enable closer study of patterns, and easily compare portions of a dataset with each other to make differences more readily apparent.	
Story Builder Plugin for CODAP	Inspired by the NSF-funded Writing Data Stories project's goal of helping middle school students become "data storytellers," the Story Builder plugin allows students to build story "moments," with each interactive moment capturing the state of a CODAP document at a given time. Since CODAP can also embed web pages and videos, a story can be truly multimedia. The plugin allows students to edit, delete, and rearrange their "moments" or lock them to prevent accidental changes. Initial work to date has shown that stories created with the Story Builder plugin are great for student projects and presentations, introductions to data-rich content, arrangements of data sequences for curriculum development, and even applications as broad as a prototype mockup environment for designing new CODAP plugin capabilities.	Information about Story Builder plugin: https://concord.org/newsletter/2021-fall/under-the-hood-three-new-codap-plugins/

continued

TABLE C-1 Continued

Case Type: Existing Tool/Software/Technology		
Case Title	*Description*	*Relevant Links/Citations*
DataBytes	Data Story Bytes or "DataBytes" describes a framework for discussing data visualizations that may appear as part of a teacher's curriculum, or in local or national news stories, with their students. These activities are designed to support quick (30 mins) discussions, in the spirit of "number talks," to critically analyze and interpret data visualizations in ways that connect to students' lives and important issues in society. Teachers can select from a series of questions designed to guide students through the following: Making sense of trends and relationships in the data or visualization, what these patterns mean, and how they connect to key science concepts. Building personal connections by considering how students' own lives and communities may be impacted by or reflected by the patterns found in data. Reflecting on the context and history of the data, how they were collected, by whom (including what gets "counted" and why), how they are visualized, what might be missing/hidden, and what questions the data can and cannot answer. Envisioning future uses of data and visualization to expand the investigation, include and explore different perspectives, and highlight the importance of understanding what's happening in the world around us in multiple ways.	Teacher guide for using Data Story Bytes: https://docs.google.com/document/d/1tAnSAZuxPKW8pigpWvjVDd8RlgH0UQ7N4DUVzceWw44/edit
Government Open Data Sets	The government is making large strides toward making open data sets findable and accessible. Along with this is a growing number of solutions to make those data sets usable. Each solution targets a different audience and, therefore, differs with regard to underlying technology, capabilities, data access strategy, and requisite skills for use. In the past, I have proposed a game to teach critical thinking approaches to problem solving. The game targets K–12 students and uses Grafana, which is open-source software that is suitable for both the needs of scientists and K–12 students as envisioned above. The primary function of Grafana is logging, but it can be adapted.	https://grafana.com/

Case Type: Real-World Application

Case Title	Description	Relevant Links/Citations
My NASA Data	The NASA My NASA Data project began in 2004 to make NASA's large collection of Earth science data accessible to K–12 students. The website now offers a number of audience-tested and proven tools for introducing data to students.	https://mynasadata.larc.nasa.gov
Invitations to Inquiry	The Invitations to Inquiry project is designed to provide short learning experiences (two to three classroom 45-minute periods) that are focused on using real-world community and citizen science data sets to make sense of a phenomenon. Students are introduced to data sets and are scaffolded through a process that helps them consider where the data come from and how they can be used to answer questions (or not). The data are hosted in FieldScope, a citizen science mapping and graphic platform, and the lessons use data from five different citizen science projects. Additionally, we have a self-paced free course for teachers to become familiar with the project, the lessons, and FieldScope. We also provide some program level resources for helping students with data (e.g., using data in discussions, introducing variables, choosing data representations). Importantly, these lessons are intended as introductory learning in data science, and they are explicitly designed to help build teacher- and student confidence in working with data. There are opportunities to go further with data in a few of the lessons (called Data+ activities).	https://bscs.org/resources/invitations-to-inquiry/

continued

TABLE C-1 Continued

Case Type: Real-World Application

Case Title	*Description*	*Relevant Links/Citations*
Meharry Data Science Summer Academy	Students, mostly from underrepresented backgrounds, learned to apply coding and data science to robotics on the Meharry Medical College campus. The students were attending the Meharry Data Science Summer Academy, funded by NASA through the Minority University Research and Education project and provided to students at no cost. NASA's goal is to support the dreams of students from traditionally underrepresented and underserved communities to enter careers in STEM. In addition to courses in programming, robotics, and data science, special sessions featured Black professionals in data science and robotics: Kenneth Harris, the deputy lead integration engineer for the NASA James Webb Telescope's Integrated Science Instrument Module Electronic Components; and Dr. Sian Proctor, the first Black woman to pilot a spacecraft. The overwhelming message was clear. A future in science and technology is within each student's grasp.	https://sacsmeharry.org/nasacamp/
Making Sense of Data: A Statistics Survival Guide	I have written a statistics guide for my high school students. I call it Making Sense of Data: A Statistics Survival Guide.	Link to statistics guide: https://drive.google.com/file/d/18EfKKZrYJdSnsMdhdzwOXWnBuw4Ivbom/view?usp=sharing
The Relationship Between Bone Density & Age in Older Females: Anatomy and Physiology Data-based Question	Strong bones are important to human health. Bone mineral density (BMD) is a way to measure how much calcium and other types of minerals are in an area of bone and helps health care providers detect bone diseases like osteoporosis and predict a person's risk for bone fractures. Biological females and the elderly are most at risk for developing osteoporosis, which is directly related to BMD. Medical researchers at the University of California, San Francisco were interested in tracking just how quickly bone density declines on average in females and how this change might vary in different bones. This kind of research is called a descriptive study. The researchers obtained (with permission) 1,886 bone density scans and age data of several hundred patients from three	Link to the full activity, including the data and citation: https://docs.google.com/document/d/18MO6avz6YrguPUO8MY8uPLU-0xLpFmiFAwSm1pn77yI/edit?usp=sharing

	clinics. The subjects were stratified into five-year age groups and BMD (g/cm2) was calculated for several skeletal areas of interest, including the lumbar spine (L1–L4), proximal radius, distal radius, and calcaneus. The researchers then converted BMD to a BMD percent relative to the 66–70 year age group.	
Indirect Estimate of Potato Cell Cytoplasm Molarity	Students use data analysis to complete an activity based on the following background (full activity included in link): Background: In 1940, botanists at The Ohio State University, Bernard Meyer and Atwell Wallace, tested two methods for indirectly determining the molarity (moles cytoplasm particles per liter of cytosol) of the solution within potato (Solanum tuberosum) cells. In general, the botanists soaked cores of potato tissue in a series of different sucrose solution strengths. The solutions were measured in osmotic pressure (atmospheres at 20°C) and ranged from 0.0 atm to 33 atm. In their study, a change of zero in length or total weight of the cores indicated that the solution in which the cores were soaked was isotonic to the potato cell cytoplasm.	Link to the full activity: https://docs.google.com/document/d/1hL4BBM46tKx7yadMmbqZojs8DCs7HQh9SA8HvANFv0U/edit?usp=sharing
Timberline High School	Timberline students in Intro to Data Science used data from our school to help determine if students who went from Algebra 2 to AP Calculus performed similarly to students who went from Precalculus to AP Calculus. Their results were used to help the school develop math pathways for all students at Timberline High School.	For more information about the math department and courses offered: https://sites.google.com/boiseschools.org/timberline-student-services/course-descriptions/math-dept?pli=1

continued

TABLE C-1 Continued

Case Type: Real-World Application		
Case Title	*Description*	*Relevant Links/Citations*
Google Map Data: A Source of "Measurement of the Distance" to Students, Traveled Paths for Supplementing Data Science Learning Activity	Students' experiences outside of the classroom, encapsulated by images, video, sound, notes, and Global Positioning System tags, can ever more easily become texts for study. Students pick distance measurements from Google Maps, and I engage them to locate two locations they have manually walked to represent the path on graph paper/board as a relationship between distance traveled and time used. Thus, students who engage in such educational data mining (picking distance from the Google map) tend to focus on using Google Maps as a tool for discovering data. This engages students to build their data and computational literacies.	Full activity can be accessed in cases document: https://www.nationalacademies.org/event/09-13-2022/docs/DC43B789C2136F62C030FAE3E7A8EB58C45EF823FACF
Transitioning from Statistics to Data Science Course in High School Setting	For the past three years, I have been working on transitioning from a traditional high school statistics course to one that uses real-world applications and daily work with SAS Studio. Thus, statistics at Perry High School has been replaced with an Intro to Data Science course. I have been very fortunate to be supported by Professor Lisa Dierker from Wesleyan University. Professor Dierker is a co-creator of Wesleyan's "Passion-Driven Statistics" model, a data-driven, project-based introductory curriculum backed by the National Science Foundation. This flexible curriculum engages students from a range of disciplines with large, real-world data sets and code-based analytic software (SAS Studio), providing experience in the rich, complicated, decision-making process of real statistical inquiry. On a daily basis, students work with current real-world data sets such as Gapminder, Nhanes, Addhealth, and Nesarc. I found the Passion-Driven Statistics model really enriched my teaching materials and student engagement.	https://www.sas.com/en_us/software/studio.html
Introduction to Data Science Activity	At the beginning of the course, the DSS classes collect data about themselves (age, height, shoe size, cotton ball toss, reaction speed, and more) to analyze throughout the course. The data collected were also geared to have a mix of quantitative and categorical data to use for different group and regression	

	models analysis. When analyzing the data, we are able the relate topics of sampling, measurement error/bias, mistakes, and outliers to real data they collected. I believe this is more powerful because it is one thing to be given a dataset and talk about measurement bias/mistakes in the data, but it is another when they are the source of the data. One example of a good discussion was "How did someone get a measurement of 8 inches for their index finger?"	
Mobile City Science	Mobile City Science (MCS) is a series of design studies of youth learning how to use data about their daily lives to make evidence-based recommendations for community change. These efforts required sometimes large groups of community stakeholders to support youth in this endeavor, including public school teachers and administrators, out-of-school time educators from libraries and museums, caregivers and families, Mayor's Office representatives, and researchers. We developed a broad design commitment to honor and elevate data collected by youth while supporting them to use tools and create data stories in forms familiar to decision makers. This design commitment came from observations and analyses of interactions between residents and urban planners that were talking, and making decisions about the future built environment, using complex spatial data visualizations.	https://www.education.uw.edu/mcs/
National Science Teaching Association (NSTA) Daily Do Playlist	There is a NSTA Daily Do Playlist of three lessons forming an instructional sequence in which students are using mathematical models (computer simulations) to explain the phenomenon of the spread of COVID-19. Students use data science and new understandings to make recommendations to keep themselves, their families, and their communities safe.	https://www.nsta.org/resources/daily-do
Fall Data Challenge	Fall Data Challenge is sponsored by the ASA. Each year, this contest challenges undergraduate and high school students to work in teams to analyze real-world data and make recommendations to combat critical issues.	https://thisisstatistics.org/FallDataChallenge/

continued

TABLE C-1 Continued

Case Type: Real-World Application

Case Title	*Description*	*Relevant Links/Citations*
Census at School	Census at School—U.S. is a free international classroom project that engages students in grades 4–12 in statistical problem solving using their own real data. Students complete an online survey, analyze their class census results, and compare their class with random samples of students in the United States and abroad.	https://ww2.amstat.org/censusatschool/
ASA Data Visualization Poster Competition	The ASA Data Visualization Poster Competition is for grades K–12 students to create a display containing two or more related graphics that summarize a set of data, look at the data from different points of view, and answer specific questions about the data.	https://www.amstat.org/education/asa-data-visualization-poster-competition-for-grades-k-12-
Hub for Innovation and Research in Statistics Education (HI-RiSE)	For many years, the projects within the Hub for Innovation and Research in Statistics Education [HI-RiSE] at NC State have worked in classrooms with students engaging them in data science activities using larger multivariate datasets in CODAP. These videos represent a sample of the successful ways students engage in data science skills and thinking within mathematics curriculum and classrooms. We use these videos to support teacher professional learning in statistics and data science.	Video 1: Students Working on the Roller Coaster Investigation https://www.youtube.com/watch?v=RvzAxKlHr0E Video 2: Discussion of the Roller Coaster Investigation https://www.youtube.com/watch?v=ETNF_542DvU Video 3: Investigating Fuel Efficiency in AP Statistics https://youtu.be/HqHiFrI6i-E
Research Projects by High School Students	In the spring of our High School Intro to Data Science class, students create their own research project. They create their own research questions and create surveys. They collect data, clean them, and analyze them using RStudio and other tools. They even use Code.org to use machine learning to create an app based on their data that will predict/classify new users. They then present their research.	https://docs.google.com/presentation/d/17rc7a1JPyU7kGSGWPrYEbXYsEIGP4sh4S5scc2SsAQc/edit?usp=sharing

Using CODAP to Tell Different Stories	Using CODAP to Tell Different Stories is an online lesson in The Statistics Teacher, a joint online publication of the ASA and the NCTM. This lesson uses the Statistical Investigation Cycle at the middle grades level to engage students in using and developing their understanding of statistics through problem solving with technological tools. Students collect data, analyze and interpret the results, as well as review the work of their peers to more deeply understand the meaning of the data and its potential implications. The problem solving and sense making using the various facets of data science provides an exceptional learning experience for students.	https://www.statisticsteacher.org/files/2021/10/Using-CODAP-to-tell-different-stories-101521_CC.pdf
GAISE II	The Guidelines for Assessment and Instruction in Statistics Education II (GAISE II) document, from the ASA and the NCTM, provides a wealth of real-world applications organized around consideration of the development of statistical thinking/data science in pre-K–12 learning.	Resources and information about GAISE: https://www.amstat.org/education/guidelines-for-assessment-and-instruction-in-statistics-education-(gaise)-reports
Strengthening Data Literacy across the Curriculum (SDLC)	Strengthening Data Literacy across the Curriculum (SDLC) studies high school mathematics curriculum modules that focus on social justice issues among students from historically marginalized groups. One module supports student analyses of income inequality in the United States using U.S. Census Bureau microdata and the online data analysis tool CODAP. As students explore these issues, they deepen their abilities to compare quantitative distributions using measures of center and variability. They also build abilities to reason with multivariable data. Based on pre- and post-module assessments and results from almost 200 students, we found statistically significant growth in students' understanding of important statistical concepts and interests in data analysis. We also found signs of greater social and political awareness and agency with data—outcomes associated with increased critical data literacy. In this module, students work through seven lessons and a final team data investigation, exploring different forms of income inequality, their scope, and possible explanations.	https://sites.google.com/view/uss-data/home

continued

TABLE C-1 Continued

Case Type: Real-World Application		
Case Title	*Description*	*Relevant Links/Citations*
Using Data Cards for Data Exploration	Using data cards for data exploration and unplugged introduction of decision trees with data with nutrition facts of food products. Children (grades 5 and 6) are asked to develop a multistep decision rule for predicting whether a food is recommendable or not. Children sort the data cards, identify reasonable split criteria, and experience the different rates of false classifications. The dependence of the decision rule on the somewhat subjective labeling and the training dataset can be experienced.	Podworny, S., Fleischer, Y., Hüsing, S., Biehler, R., Frischemeier, D., Höper, L., and Schulte, C. (2021). Using data cards for teaching data based decision trees in middle school. *21st Koli Calling International Conference on Computing Education Research* (Koli Calling '21), Joensuu, Finland. ACM. https://doi.org/10.1145/3488042.3489966
High School Machine Learning Teaching Module Development	This paper reports on progress in the development of a teaching module on machine learning with decision trees for secondary-school students, in which students use survey data about media use of youth to predict who plays online games frequently (to suggest specific advertisements for online games to these students). The dataset consists of more than 500 cases and more than 50 variables and is also used for just data exploration activities as a preparatory step before introducing machine learning. They use CODAP's "Arbor" plugin to manually build decision trees and understand how to systematically build trees based on data. Further on, the students use a menu-based environment in a Jupyter Notebook to apply an algorithm that automatically generates decision trees and to evaluate and optimize the performance of these. Students acquire technical and conceptual skills but also reflect on personal and social aspects of the uses of algorithms from machine learning.	Biehler, R., and Fleischer, Y. (2021). Introducing students to machine learning with decision trees using CODAP and Jupyter Notebooks. *Teaching Statistics, 43*(S1), S133–S142. https://doi.org/10.1111/test.12279

Introduction to Data Science for Secondary School Students	In this paper, we will describe an introduction to data science for secondary school students. We will report on the design and implementation of an introductory unit on "data and data detectives with CODAP" in which secondary school students used the online tool CODAP to explore real and meaningful survey data on leisure time activities and media use (so-called JIM-PB data) in a statistical project setting as a starting point for data science. The JIM-PB dataset served as a valuable dataset that offered meaningful and exciting opportunities for data exploration for secondary school students, and CODAP proved to be a valuable tool for the first explorations of these data.	Frischemeier, D., Biehler, R., Podworny, S., and Budde, L. (2021). A first introduction to data science education in secondary schools: Teaching and learning about data exploration with CODAP using survey data. *Teaching Statistics, 43*(S1), S182–S189. https://doi.org/10.1111/test.12283
NetApp Data Explorers	NetApp Data Explorers is an after-school program, funded by NetApp, that introduces middle school students to data science in the context of "using data for social good." Data Explorers focuses on the 17 United Nations Sustainable Development Goals (SDGs), which present a "blueprint to achieve a better and more sustainable future for all," and introduces participants to the data the United Nations has collected to track progress in the SDGs. Using CODAP, students explore health and education indicators from 195 countries that belong to the United Nations. While Data Explorers has been very engaging for participants in its pilot phases in the United States, England, and the Netherlands, we have also identified some challenges in the process of implementing (and revising) the program. For example, while middle school students are especially attuned to issues of "social good" and inequity, it is a big leap from noticing, for example, that African countries have lower life expectancies to coming up with a sensible and realistic "call to action." In addition, much of the data is reported as rates (e.g., number of doctors per 100,000 people in a country), which may be mathematically challenging for some students to understand. Finally, all of these kinds of "civic data" are aggregated across a country, county, or other political entity; this kind of aggregation disguises a lot of local variability so runs contrary to many youths' experience, which tends to be at much smaller geographical scale, like a neighborhood.	https://www.netapp.com/social-impact/data-science-education/

continued

TABLE C-1 Continued

Case Type: Real-World Application		
Case Title	*Description*	*Relevant Links/Citations*
Data Jam/Puerto Rico	Data Jam/Puerto Rico is a five-year-long project in Puerto Rico to introduce middle and high school students to data science by engaging them in authentic environmental investigations using long-term ecological datasets. Students engaged in Data Jam/Puerto Rico are provided access to decades of long-term ecological data from El Yunque National Forest gathered by the Luquillo Long-Term Ecological Research (LTER) program at the University of Puerto Rico. After a series of introductory activities, students work in teams to come up with a research question, analyze the data using CODAP, and use the evidence from their analyses to answer their research question. Some of the groups present their posters at an annual Data Jam Symposium. The project team's primary activities are providing professional development for the participating teachers (most of whom teach either science or math), supporting teachers in classroom implementation through a combination of educational materials and classroom visits, and curating data sets from the LTER so that they are possible for students to use. In this last task, the team has been supported by a data fellow funded by the Environmental Data Initiative (EDI). The intervention also includes several scientific mentors, young Puerto Rican scientists who serve as role models for students by sharing their career paths and advising them on their data analysis.	General information about DataJam: https://lternet.edu/data-jams/ https://czo-archive.criticalzone.org/luquillo/education-outreach/k-12-education-luquillo/

Financial Literacy: Retirement Calculations	Students decide on a retirement age (my students used age 65) to calculate their age until retirement. They decide on two amounts they think they could save per week—one realistic, one a stretch—and everyone uses those amounts for comparison purposes. They use TheMint.org's compounding calculator to figure amounts until retirement if that weekly money (calculated to yearly savings) is invested in a savings account (0.50% return) or the stock market (7% return, historically). Next, they collect and share those data in either an online spreadsheet or a paper graph. Students make predictions about how weekly savings amounts translate across time and investment vehicle. Some students multiply by 48 weeks instead of 52, so there are opportunities for conversations there. (Also requires conversations around unpredictability of stock market as well as how fees, buying and selling, etc. affect growth.) Students who initially said they had NO money to invest usually are thinking by the end of the activity about how much they could spare per week. MATH STANDARD: Represent and analyze quantitative relationships between dependent and independent variables. EXTENSION ACTIVITY: Calculate how much money a person could save if they had a better credit rating on a vehicle loan or a house mortgage. Take the difference in those two amounts and have students see how much that could equate to if it was invested and compounded over time.	https://themint.org/~theminto/kids/compounding-calculator.html

continued

TABLE C-1 Continued

Case Type: Real-World Application		
Case Title	*Description*	*Relevant Links/Citations*
DataJam	Pittsburgh DataWorks, along with the West Big Data Innovation Hub and the New York Hall of Science, developed a virtualized version of the DataJam, an annual program and competition for high school students that runs throughout the academic year and introduces youth to data visualization and analytic skills to answer a research question of their own design. DataJam mentors—volunteer university undergraduate students trained in mentorship, statistics, data ethics, and community-based research principles—guide students. The COVID-19 pandemic forced us to migrate DataJam to 100% online for the 2021–22 school year. We piloted an online format to expand the program to culturally and geographically diverse teams and an eMentoring model. This provides us with an opportunity to determine how to expand, scale, and replicate the success of DataJam to reach the most underserved communities that lack access to the resources and expertise to participate in rich data science programs. We expanded DataJam participation to high schools across Pennsylvania, New Jersey, and Massachusetts, and the Pala Native American Tribal lands in Southern California through videoconferencing and other online collaboration tools. Focus groups and surveys conducted with the students and teachers showed that the program was successful online in very diverse cultural and geographical settings. We hope to explore expanding the diversity of high school participants to include underserved urban, rural, immigrant, unhoused, and tribal youth, and to deepen our understanding of the factors that lead to changes in self-efficacy and career aspirations in the target youth.	https://www.pghdataworks.org/data-jam

Impact of Introducing Data Science to Students on Major/Degree Choice	My background is pediatrics, immunology, and medical informatics. I have a profound experience of using ontology for data integration and data analysis in health and regulatory areas. I have been mentoring junior high schoolers and college students to work on Food and Drug Administration–funded informatics projects or university collaborative research projects. Out of four female (all minority background) students, three switched their major or chose the major in data science or information technology. One of them switched from pre-med to a data science track. I keep mentoring those students who are currently in college majoring in data science for continuous data science research.	
StoryQ	The NSF-funded StoryQ project, aimed at providing opportunities for youth to use data science and AI to explore language-centered scenarios, represents a successful real-world application of data science. One example of this application engages students in using a data-focused view to analyze poetry. Students process poetry to identify and characterize features of its language such as the number and type of syllables in each line, then use patterns uncovered in the data to develop and train a machine learning model in the StoryQ app, a plugin to CODAP. The goal of the curriculum is to scaffold text analytics for English Language Arts students, so they learn to understand and appreciate both poetry and applications of data and AI. Data analysis lies doubly at the heart of the StoryQ activities, as students not only use analysis to examine and identify patterns in language to train a model but also use data visualization and analysis to evaluate the results of the model, directly evaluating the weights of various parameters derived from applying their model in order to characterize the text itself as well as to judge the accuracy of the model. In this manner, StoryQ stands as an example of the ways students can use data analysis as a tool both to shed new light on traditional school subjects and as a pathway toward understanding new applications of data and computing.	https://www.nsf.gov/awardsearch/showAward?AWD_ID=1949110

continued

TABLE C-1 Continued

Case Type: Real-World Application		
Case Title	*Description*	*Relevant Links/Citations*
Maize High School	Biology students at Maize High School conducted primary water quality sampling in partnership with the United States Geological Survey—Kansas (USGS-KS) in 2018 to develop a predictive model for the occurrence of harmful algal blooms in Cheney Reservoir, the primary drinking water supply for Wichita, Kansas and surrounding communities. The students working on this project ALL became STEM majors at universities across the United States, and the teacher was contracted by Microsoft as a big data analyst. She wrote FarmBeats for Students machine learning and AI curricula for Future Farmers of America (FFA) and Center for Agriculture Science Education (CASE), and helped to develop the machine learning methodologies being deployed across all industries.	
New Data Science Course for High Schoolers	In our state, we had a success in data science with youth as we developed a course for high schoolers based upon data science, and offered a course for which students could receive either math or computer science credit. A lot of time and research went in to developing this course, and we believe it highlights the changes in education, and the importance of computer science and data science in today's education.	
The Next Grand Challenge: Building Critical Mass for Data Science	The California Education Learning Lab is pleased to announce the release of a new grant opportunity to promote the buildout of critical data science educational infrastructure. Through this request for proposal, Learning Lab's Grand Challenge seeks to incentivize public higher education institutions to embrace data science as an opportunity to build new pathways, modernize majors, attract historically underrepresented students into STEM, and deepen both civic and interdisciplinary learning.	https://calearninglab.org/ https://calearninglab.org/grant/data-science-rfp/